hsa*ba

စားပါ အားမနာပါနဲ့။

Burmese Cookbook

Tin Cho Chaw

www.hsaba.com

For my mother, Amy

First published in 2008 by Grassblades Ltd.

This edition published in 2013 by
Chosillano Ferrente
Suite 471 Kemp House,
152 City Road, London EC1V 2NX

www.hsaba.com

A catalogue record for this book is
available from the British Library

ISBN 978-0-9559374-1-5

Printed in China

contents

introduction

It is one of those perfect evenings, golden beams cast shadows across the grass as the sun plays hide and seek between the trees. The heat of the day is slowly tamed by an increasing breeze, bringing with it the gentle fragrance of jasmine from the garden. It is times like this when I long for recipes like Burmese curry (*sipyan*), a wonderfully versatile dish, which works all year round. For mild summer evenings, the curry tossed with noodles and a fresh tangy dressing makes a light and tasty supper. The distinct flavour of the curry comes from the slow cooking of the onion, garlic and chillies, sending wafts of sweet aroma through the kitchen as the mixture starts to caramelise. There is little to do except to allow the meat to simmer and become beautifully tender.

This is what I love about Burmese cooking: it's easy and straightforward, it uses familiar ingredients and uncomplicated recipes that translate well into everyday cooking.

The idea for hsa*ba began when I noticed that over the course of many years living away from Burma, my family had altered recipes and replaced ingredients that were hard to find. I wanted to strip away these adaptations and return to real home-cooked Burmese food. This took me on a journey back to Burma with my husband, Christopher, to rediscover the food my family cooked and ate when I was growing up in Rangoon.

During our visit, we spent many hours in the small kitchen of my Aunt Bee's house, on the second floor, watching and cooking with my cousins. It was alive with the sounds of a pestle striking a stone mortar and a simmering wok of duck and potato on a charcoal stove. Mid-afternoons, we drank sweet thick avocado shakes and ate sticky rice in ice-cold coconut milk to refresh ourselves and cool off. We photographed the food just before we sat down to eat. This inspired me to capture and share the essence of a Burmese kitchen, and the unspoken secrets that make a particular dish outstanding.

This book contains 100 treasured recipes collected from my family, such as the much-loved Traditional fish noodle soup (*mohingar*), Burmese chicken biryani (*dan bauk*) and Festive duck noodle soup (*kaw yea khaut swe*). These I tend to think of as weekend food — meals that are best enjoyed with family and friends. I have included many of my favourites: fresh yet robust salads (*thote*) that make a quick weekday lunch or supper; hearty one-pot dishes requiring little effort yet producing beautiful results; and recipes with a hint of Chinese or Indian influence. I prefer to serve several dishes, as we do in Burma, and have included 'eat with' suggestions to help you put together a balanced menu.

A meal would not be complete without something sweet to end with. The moist Golden semolina pudding (*shwegyi sanwei makin*) and the indulgent Burmese faluda (*paluda*) make excellent desserts. Other sweet treats like caramelised crispy pancakes, sticky rice with coconut and many more are great as teatime snacks. If any ingredients are difficult to buy outside Burma, I have tried to suggest the next best thing. And if you are new to Asian cooking, there is a glossary of ingredients on www.hsaba.com, which should make the process less daunting.

Enjoy using these recipes, feel free to be playful with the flavours and make them your own. Most importantly hsaba, please eat.

savoury snacks

pea crackers

ပဲကြော် | pe kyaw

On the streets of Rangoon, there are many food stalls that sell an assortment of tempting crispy crunchy fritters. The ones I particularly like are the golden discs of pea crackers. They are broken into pieces and sprinkled on top of Traditional fish noodle soup (page 132). I also think they make a tasty snack on their own with a spicy chilli dip.

ingredients
60g yellow split peas, soaked overnight with ¼ teaspoon baking soda
25g rice flour
100ml water
a small pinch of ground turmeric
½ teaspoon salt
peanut oil for frying

method
Put the rice flour in a bowl then slowly mix in the water to form a loose batter. Add the yellow split peas, turmeric and salt. Mix well until they are all nicely combined.

Heat the oil in a frying pan. There should be just enough to coat the bottom of the pan. Take a tablespoon of the mixture and carefully ladle it into the pan to form a disc. As the batter is very thin the oil will spit a little. To make sure all of the crackers have a consistent texture give the batter a good stir and try to include an even amount of peas every time you ladle the batter into the pan. Fry the fritters over moderate heat in batches of 4 or 5, depending on the size of the pan. Replenish the oil if necessary.

After 2-3 minutes, the edges will be golden and the fritters will stiffen so that you can easily flip them over using a spatula. Fry the other side for a minute or so until they are golden brown. Remove with a slotted spoon and drain on kitchen paper.

makes: 15-20 crackers
cooking time: 20 mins

variations
I sometimes shred a few fresh curry leaves and add them to the batter which makes the crackers very aromatic.

eat with
Traditional fish noodle soup ... p132
Coconut noodle soup ... p142
Sour chilli dip ... p201

yellow split pea fritters

ဘယာကြော် | baya kyaw

These fritters regularly feature as an appetiser when a group of friends come over for dinner. They are so easy to make and popular with everyone. I usually pile them on a plate with a spicy sour dip and watch them disappear in minutes. On rare occasions when there are leftovers, they make a quick lunch stuffed in naan bread with chilli sauce and salad.

ingredients

250g dried yellow split peas, soaked overnight
1 medium onion, finely chopped
handful of fresh coriander, finely chopped
1 red chilli, finely chopped
¼ teaspoon paprika
¼ teaspoon ground turmeric
1 teaspoon salt
peanut oil for deep frying

method

First prepare the onion, chilli and coriander by chopping them finely, then leave on one side.

Drain the peas and blitz half in a food processor to a coarse consistency, then tip into a bowl. Blitz the remaining half to a smooth paste, adding a little water (no more than 1 tablespoon) to help it along. Mix the two batches together. This will give the fritters a good texture and will stop them splitting during the frying process.

Mix in the chopped onion, chilli, coriander, spices and salt. Make sure all the ingredients are evenly incorporated.

Heat enough oil in a saucepan to deep fry (never fill the pan more than halfway). Scoop a teaspoon of the mixture and work with another teaspoon to form a bite-sized oval shape. Gently drop the fritters one by one into the oil. Deep fry in batches of 6 to 8 fritters on moderate heat. After 2-4 minutes they will turn golden brown.

Remove with a slotted spoon and drain on kitchen paper. They are best served warm with sour chilli or tamarind dip.

makes: 30-35 fritters
cooking time: 20-30 mins

tip

They can be made in advance and frozen until needed. When frying the fritters, remove from the oil when they are just beginning to turn golden. Let them cool completely before freezing. When needed, defrost and place under a hot grill for 2-4 minutes on each side to warm through and make them crisp again.

variations
Here's another way to serve these fritters: cut them in half and toss in a salad dressing of lemon juice, fish sauce and sliced onions.

eat with
Sour chilli dip ... p201
Tamarind dip ... p204
Naan bread ... p20

marinated pork skewers
ဝက်သားမီးကင် | wet thar mekin

When we visited my cousin in Rangoon, he made these pork skewers grilled on a small charcoal stove. I think this recipe is typically Burmese: a fusion of influences from neighbouring countries. They make an excellent appetiser or snack, served with a tart soy sauce dip and perfect for throwing on the barbecue.

marinade
1cm fresh ginger, sliced
3 garlic cloves
2 lemon grass stalks, white part only
1 large red chilli
1 tablespoon fish sauce
1 tablespoon peanut oil
1 teaspoon sugar
2 tablespoons rice wine or dry sherry
1 teaspoon garam masala

450g fatty pork, cut into small chunks
12 bamboo skewers, soaked in water for 1 hour

method
Soak the bamboo skewers in a bowl of water to ensure the ends do not burn on the grill. Put the pork in a small bowl. Using a pestle and mortar, pound the ginger, garlic, lemon grass and chilli, then add the remaining ingredients and mix well. Pour the marinade over the meat, cover and leave in the fridge for an hour.

When you are ready to cook the meat, thread 3-5 pieces of meat onto each skewer. Pop onto a barbecue or under a preheated grill for 15-20 minutes, turning occasionally until cooked through. I like to let the meat catch some colour to give it that wonderful char-grilled flavour.

serves: 4
cooking time: 20 mins

eat with
Soy sauce dip ... p201

fish cakes

ငါးဖယ်ခြော့ | nga hpe kyaw

These simple fish cakes are versatile. They can be served with a dip or sliced and added to a thote (Burmese style salad), such as Mandalay noodle salad (page 146) and Hand-mixed salad (page 138), to give extra flavour and texture.

ingredients
450g white fish, skinned and boned
1 small onion, finely chopped
1 red chilli, finely chopped
2 tablespoons plain flour
¼ teaspoon salt
peanut oil for frying

method
Cut the fish into manageable pieces. Using a pestle and mortar, pound for 10-15 minutes until it becomes a smooth sticky paste. You can also use a food processor to do this. Mix in the onion, chilli and flour.

To form the fish cakes, have a bowl of water ready to moisten your fingers so the mixture doesn't stick to your hands. Take a small handful of the mixture, roll into a ball and flatten with the palms of your hands. Each fish cake should be about 5cm in diameter and 1cm thick.

Shallow fry the fish cakes, in batches, for 2-3 minutes on each side until they are golden brown. Remove from the oil and drain on kitchen paper. Serve them warm with sour chilli dip.

makes: 10-12 cakes
cooking time: 30 mins

tip
If you want to serve the fish cakes as finger food, make them smaller, about 2-3cm in diameter.

variations
This recipe can also be used to make fish balls for 12 ingredient soup (page 192). Divide the mixture into 20 portions and roll each portion into a ball. Pop them into a pan of boiling water. Cover and simmer for 2-3 minutes. When the fish balls are cooked, they will float to the top. Remove with a slotted spoon and drain.

eat with
Sour chilli dip ... p201
Mandalay noodle salad ... p146
Hand-mixed salad ... p138

sprouted peas & crispy onions

ပဲပြုပ်ကြော် | pe pyote kyaw

I use chickpeas for this recipe as it's rather difficult to find vatana peas, which are used in Burma. Don't be put off by the sprouting process; there is little to do except to keep the peas moist by rinsing them twice a day and waiting for the shoots to emerge.

ingredients
250g dried chickpeas
350ml water
½ tablespoon peanut oil
1 teaspoon salt
¼ teaspoon baking soda
¼ teaspoon ground turmeric

garnish
1 onion, made into crispy onions
(page 206)

method
To sprout the chickpeas, remove any broken or damaged peas before soaking in water for 8 hours. I usually leave them overnight. It's simple to make your own sprouting container. I use a large bowl, a sieve or colander that will fit inside the bowl, a piece of muslin cloth and a large plate or lid that will cover the bowl.

Line the sieve with the cloth and tip in the drained chickpeas. Rinse under the tap until the peas and the cloth are soaked. Drain off excess water then place the sieve in the bowl. Pull over the corners of the cloth and put a plate or lid on top.

The key is to keep the peas moist, away from direct sunlight and at a cool temperature. Rinse the peas at least twice a day to make sure they do not dry out and die. As sprouts begin to develop, gently shake after rinsing to remove excess water so they don't go mouldy. After 2-3 days, the sprouts should be about 2-3cm in length and ready for cooking.

Put the sprouted peas in a large saucepan, add the remaining ingredients and bring to the boil. I usually add the baking soda as this helps to reduce the cooking time. Cover the pan and simmer on moderate heat for 40-50 minutes. The peas are ready when all the water has been absorbed and they are soft.

Just before serving I like to add crispy onions and a dash of fish sauce. The peas can be eaten as they are with rice or naan bread.

serves: 4
cooking time: 55 mins

tip
If you want to miss out the sprouting process, just cook the chickpeas straight after soaking.

eat with
Burmese stir-fried rice ... p168
Naan bread ... p20

naan bread

 | nan pyar

This is my husband's version of naan bread. Although not a traditional Burmese recipe, it goes so well with Sprouted peas & crispy onions I thought I had to share it. Spelt flour is used which gives them a lovely springy, chewy texture. It's also great for mopping up a curry and dunking in red lentil soup.

ingredients
½ teaspoon yeast
1 teaspoon sugar
½ teaspoon salt
50ml tepid milk
150ml tepid water
350g white spelt flour

method
Mix the yeast and sugar in a glass and add 50ml of water. Let it stand for 10 minutes until frothy. Put the flour and salt in a mixing bowl, make a well in the middle and pour in the yeast mixture. Pour in the milk and water. Stir with a fork until it comes together. If the dough is too sticky add a little more flour until it becomes a soft dough. Turn out onto a lightly floured surface and knead for 5 minutes. With spelt flour you mustn't over-knead.

Cover with a cloth and prove for 1 hour at room temperature until the dough has doubled in size. Knock back the dough by lifting it and divide into 6 portions. Roll each portion into a ball and place on an oven tray and cover with a cloth. Prove for another 30-45 minutes until doubled in size again.

When the dough is ready for baking, preheat the grill on high heat. Take each ball and roll out into an oval shape, about ½cm in thickness. Pop onto a lightly floured oven tray and cook under the grill, in batches for about 2 minutes on each side until the naan has puffed up and some of the top is slightly charred. Drizzle some melted butter over them and serve immediately.

makes: 6
cooking time: 20 mins, not including proving

tip
We sometimes double the recipe and then only lightly grill half the naans. Once cooled these can be popped in the freezer. When you need them again just put under a hot grill when still frozen and heat through.

eat with
Sprouted peas & crispy onions ... p19
Chicken masala ... p42
Red lentil soup ... p183

crispy fritter batter

 | a kyaw

Crispy gourd or onion fritters are essential garnishes for Traditional fish noodle soup (page 132). They can also be eaten on their own with a chilli dip as a starter. My grandmother used to say anything fried or thote (Burmese style salad) tastes good. So she would treat us to the best of both and make onion fritters thote with tamarind juice and fish sauce.

ingredients
4 tablespoons ground rice flour
4 tablespoons self-raising flour
1 tablespoon sticky/glutinous rice flour
1 tablespoon chickpea flour
¼ teaspoon baking powder
½ teaspoon salt
1 tablespoon peanut oil
75ml ice cold water
peanut oil for deep frying

1 large onion, sliced lengthways, or
200g gourd, sliced into 1cm thick strips (you can also use marrow or courgette)

method
Put all the dry ingredients in a mixing bowl and add the oil. Stirring continuously, add the cold water a little at a time until incorporated. Leave the batter in the fridge to rest for 30 minutes. Meanwhile prepare the vegetables for frying.

A deep-fat fryer is ideal but if you don't have one, heat the oil in a medium-sized saucepan (never fill the pan more than halfway). When the oil is hot, dip the gourd in the batter just before you drop it into the oil. For the onion fritters, put a small handful of the onion into the batter, coat it well then spoon into the oil.

Deep fry in batches for 5-10 minutes or until golden brown, turning occasionally. Drain on kitchen paper and serve while still warm.

makes: 18-20 fritters
cooking time: 30 mins

tip
If you don't have any sticky rice flour or chickpea flour, you can leave them out. Instead use 5 tablespoons rice flour and 5 tablespoons self-raising flour.

variations
Add a pinch of turmeric and paprika to the batter mixture for a bit of colour and spice.

eat with
Sour chilli dip ... p201
Traditional fish noodle soup ... p132

potato cutlets stuffed with lamb

အာလူးကက်သလစ် | aloo kuttelet

This is a snack which is Indian in origin; fluffy mashed potato stuffed with spicy minced lamb and green peas. Eat hot with a dollop of minty yoghurt dip.

ingredients

650g floury potatoes, unpeeled
½ teaspoon salt
handful of fresh mint, finely chopped
1 egg, beaten
plain flour for dusting
peanut oil for frying

filling

3 tablespoons peanut oil
½ onion, finely chopped
1 garlic clove, finely chopped

¼ teaspoon turmeric
¼ teaspoon paprika
¼ teaspoon ground coriander
¼ teaspoon ground cumin
½ teaspoon garam masala
2 green chillies, chopped
50g green peas
100g minced lamb
100ml water
salt & black pepper

method

Drop the potatoes into a pan full of salted water. Bring to the boil and simmer on low heat for 20-25 minutes, until they are tender but not falling apart or cracked. Drain and cool enough so you can peel the skins. Mash them with a fork and mix in the salt and mint.

While the potatoes are cooking, make the filling. Heat the oil in a saucepan and cook the onion and garlic for 5-10 minutes until soft and transparent. Add the spices and chillies, cook until fragrant, then add the minced lamb. Give it a quick stir and pour in the water. Bring to the boil and simmer for 15-20 minutes until all the water has evaporated and the meat is tender. Stir in the peas and cook a further minute. Season with salt and black pepper.

When you are ready to make the cutlets, dust your hands with some flour, take a small handful of the mashed potato and form a round ball about 4cm in diameter. Pop the ball onto a square of cling film and flatten with the palm of your hand. Place a heaped teaspoon of the lamb mixture in the middle and scoop up the four corners of the cling film to envelope the filling with the potato. Seal the top of the ball with your fingers and reshape to form a cutlet.

Heat a thin layer of oil in a large, non-stick frying pan. Dip each cutlet in some flour and shake off any excess before dipping into the beaten egg. Pop straight into the oil and fry over medium heat for about 5 minutes on each side until golden brown. Remove with a slotted spoon and drain on kitchen paper.

makes: 10-12 cutlets
cooking time: 45-55 mins

eat with

Minty yoghurt sauce ... p210

ginger salad
ရင်းသုတ် | ghin thote

This is best made with very young ginger which has thin, almost transparent skin and is slightly pink. Pickling the ginger is straightforward - just leave in the fridge for a couple of days before it's ready to eat. The Ginger salad makes a good digestive served after a meal. I think it's also a great snack to bridge the gap between lunch and dinner!

ingredients
35g fresh young ginger, thinly sliced on a mandolin
3 tablespoons rice vinegar or lime juice
2 teaspoons sugar
125ml peanut oil
2 small shallots, thinly sliced
5 garlic cloves, sliced
35g chana dal (or yellow split peas)
¼ teaspoon baking soda
35g unsalted peanuts, roasted
1 tablespoon sesame seeds, toasted
1 teaspoon dried shrimps, pounded into floss
2 green chillies, sliced
1 teaspoon fish sauce
½ lime, juiced

method
Make the pickled ginger. Put the vinegar and sugar in a small saucepan. Heat gently until the sugar is dissolved. Remove from the heat and cool a little before pouring over the ginger. Make sure it's well coated, cover and leave in the fridge for 2 days.

The night before making the salad, soak the chana dal in a bowl of water with the baking soda. The next day, drain and pat dry thoroughly with kitchen paper.

Heat the oil in a saucepan and fry the shallots until golden. Remove from the oil and drain on kitchen paper. Do the same for the garlic and chana dal. When all the fried ingredients are cool, they will become crisp. Reserve 1 tablespoon of the frying oil for the salad dressing.

When the ginger is ready, drain and squeeze with your hands to remove any liquid, then cut into matchsticks. In a bowl, mix together the pickled ginger, fried ingredients, roasted peanuts, sesame seeds, dried shrimps and green chillies. Mix in the dressing: 1 tablespoon of frying oil, fish sauce and lime juice. Serve in small bowls.

serves: 6-8
cooking time: 20 mins

shrimp & bean sprout cups

ပုဇွန်ခွက်ကြော် | pazoon gwet kyaw

What I love about these fritters is that they are crispy, especially the edges where the bean sprouts stick out, but soft and moist in the middle. They can be eaten hot, with a tamarind dip, or made into a crispy salad: cut the fritters into quarters and toss with sliced red onions, cucumber, fresh coriander, a drizzle of garlic oil, tamarind juice and fish sauce.

ingredients
200g fresh bean sprouts, washed and drained
100g shelled shrimps
1 medium onion, thinly sliced
60g rice flour
35g chickpea flour
1 tablespoon cornflour
1 teaspoon salt
200ml cold water
peanut oil for deep frying

method
Make the batter. Put the rice flour, chickpea flour, corn flour and salt in a bowl. Mix in the cold water slowly while stirring to form a batter. The consistency should be similar to single cream. Leave in the fridge while you wash the bean sprouts and prepare the shrimps. When you are ready to make the fritters, put the bean sprouts in a tea towel and pat them to ensure they are completely dry. Add them to the batter along with the sliced onions and shrimps.

Pour enough oil in a saucepan for deep frying (making sure not to fill more than halfway). Place a ladle into the hot oil for a minute to warm. Then empty it leaving a little oil at the bottom of the ladle.

Quickly spoon the mixture into the ladle and lower into the oil. Leave the ladle in the oil for a couple of minutes until the top is beginning to brown. Using a spoon, carefully tease out the fritter. Cook for a further 3-4 minutes on the other side until the fritter is golden brown all over. Remove from the oil with a slotted spoon and drain on kitchen paper. Repeat this process of frying one fritter at a time.

makes: 8 fritters
cooking time: 45 mins

tip
The ladle method makes the fritters cup-shaped. This can be a little tricky and time-consuming as each fritter is fried individually. Alternatively just spoon a generous tablespoon of the mixture straight into the oil and fry in batches until golden brown.

eat with
Tamarind dip ... p204

pumpkin & shrimp cake
ကင်ကွာကိပ် | kim kuat kait

August is the time of year when pumpkins are in season in Burma. We all look forward to eating kim kuat kait which my mother makes in vast quantities. Some we eat fresh straight from the steamer and the rest we save for another day. I sometimes use butternut squash as the caramelised onions and the sweetness of the butternut work really well. This makes an excellent appetiser or mid-afternoon snack, served with sour chilli dip.

ingredients
1 large onion, sliced lengthways
250g ground rice
½ tablespoon cornflour
250ml water (to soak rice)
450g peeled pumpkin, cut into 2cm cubes
large handful of dried shrimps
1 teaspoon salt
peanut oil to fry onions

method
Pour the ground rice into a large bowl. Mix in the cornflour and water. Cover with cling film and leave to soak while preparing the remaining ingredients. Heat enough oil in a small saucepan to deep fry the onions. As they begin to turn golden, remove with a slotted spoon and drain on kitchen paper. You may need to fry the onions in batches. Keep the cooked onion oil for later use.

Next put the chopped pumpkin into a pan and pour over enough water so it is just covering the pumpkin. Bring to the boil and simmer for 10-15 minutes until tender. Drain and keep the pumpkin water for later use.

Soak the dried shrimps in hot water for 5 minutes. Drain and squeeze any remaining water from the shrimps with your hands. In a frying pan, pour a tablespoon of the onion oil and fry the shrimps on high heat for 2 minutes. This will help to release their smoky pungent flavour. Remove from the heat and set aside.

Mash the pumpkin thoroughly with a potato masher and add the soaked ground rice, fried shrimps, two thirds of the fried onions and salt. Also add 4 tablespoons of the onion oil and 100ml of boiled pumpkin water. Mix well, turning the mixture into a pale orange/yellow colour.

Grease 2 containers, approximately 17cm x 12cm x 6cm, with a little onion oil and pour the mixture three quarters of the way up in each. Sprinkle the remaining fried onions over the top and gently press into the mixture so it is level.

Place in a steamer for 45-55 minutes. When done, the texture of the cakes should be firm and springy to the touch and they should come away from the sides easily. Let the cakes cool a little so it can be handled and cut into slices.

serves: 6-8
cooking time: 60-90 mins

tip
Each cake will serve 4 people as an appetiser. If using from frozen, defrost and cut into bite-sized chunks. Fry in a little oil until golden brown and the sides are crispy.

eat with
Sour chilli dip ... p201
Tamarind dip ... p204

chargrilled chicken wings

 | kyet thar mekin

A very easy marinade - just throw all the ingredients together and rub into any chosen meat. I think it works particularly well with chicken wings as they make a moreish finger food, perfect for a summer barbecue.

marinade
1 tablespoon shrimp paste
4 tablespoons hot water
1 tablespoon honey
1 tablespoon peanut oil
1 teaspoon fermented bean curd
1 lime, juiced
12 chicken wings, tips removed

method
Put the shrimp paste in a small bowl. Mix in the hot water and work with a fork to form a runny paste. Add the remaining ingredients and stir well. Pour the marinade over the chicken and leave covered in the fridge for at least an hour.

Place the chicken wings on a barbecue for 5 minutes on each side, brushing with any leftover marinade as they cook. If they are colouring too quickly, move to the side of the barbecue where there is less heat. Pierce with a skewer to see if the juices run clear.

Alternatively, they can be cooked in a preheated oven set to 200°C/400°F/Gas6. Pop the chicken wings on an oven tray and roast for 20-30 minutes, occasionally basting with the marinade and its own juices. Again cook until the juices run clear.

serves: 4
cooking time: 15-35 mins

Off the main road, down a small muddy track, we stumbled upon a few houses where piles of tea leaves were left on bamboo mats to dry in the open air. This reminded me of pickled tea leaves (laphet), one of my favourite nibbles.

Laphet is essentially green tea. The young leaves are plucked, steamed and buried underground from four to seven months for the fermentation process to take place. When the pickled tea leaves are ready, they are eaten with crispy garlic, sesame seeds, roasted peanuts, dried shrimps, fried butter beans and chana dal.

Traditionally laphet is served when we receive visitors, in an elaborately decorated lacquerware with different compartments to house each ingredient. A little of each crispy titbit and laphet are spooned straight into the mouth and savoured slowly, sometimes with a bite of raw garlic and green chilli. A cup of hot tea completes the ritual.

For those new to laphet, I premix the salad, tossing in a little onion oil, diced tomato then season with a squeeze of lime juice and a dash of fish sauce. This salad makes a great appetiser served with a cool glass of beer to whet the appetite.

pickled tea leaf salad
လက်ဖက်သုတ် | laphet thote

There are several brands and types of laphet sold in packets, usually available from a Burmese supplier. Ask for the plain pickled tea leaves which have whole leaves and no other ingredients added. Laphet has a unique and gentle bitter taste. Well worth a try!

ingredients
1 tablespoon pickled tea leaves
125ml peanut oil
5 garlic cloves, sliced
30g chana dal (or yellow split peas)
30g dried butter beans
20g unsalted peanuts, roasted
1 tablespoon sesame seeds, toasted
1 teaspoon dried shrimps, pounded into floss
2 green chillies, sliced
1 tomato, chopped
1 teaspoon fish sauce
½ lime, juiced

method
Soak both the chana dal and butter beans in separate bowls of water for 8 hours or overnight. Drain and pat dry thoroughly with kitchen paper.

Heat the oil in a saucepan and fry the garlic until golden. Remove from the oil and drain on kitchen paper. Do the same for the chana dal and butter beans. Reserve 1 tablespoon of the frying oil.

When all the fried ingredients are cool, put them in a bowl and add the pickled tea leaves and the remaining ingredients. Mix with a tablespoon of the frying oil. Taste and adjust seasoning as you wish. I like to add a dash more lime.

serves: 4-6
cooking time: 20 mins

meat & poultry

chicken curry

ကြက်သားဆီပြန် | kyet thar sipyan

Curry in Burmese is sipyan which literally means 'oil returns', a sign when the gravy is ready. Rather than using spices, this recipe relies on the chicken and the fried onions to flavour the curry. I always use an organic chicken and cook it on the bone so the gravy takes on the full flavour of the meat.

ingredients
½ teaspoon ground turmeric
½ teaspoon salt
3 tablespoons fish sauce
1 whole chicken, jointed into 8 pieces, or 8 thighs and/or drumsticks
2 medium onions, thinly sliced
4 garlic cloves, crushed
1 teaspoon crushed dried chillies
125ml peanut oil
500ml water

method
Mix the ground turmeric, salt and fish sauce in a bowl. Add the chicken and toss in the marinade. Leave for 30 minutes while you cook the fried onions.

Heat the oil in a saucepan and fry the onions in batches until they are just beginning to turn lightly golden. Remove from the oil and leave to one side. In the same oil, lightly brown the chicken on all sides. This is important as it will give the curry a wonderful flavour. Remove the chicken from the pan and set aside.

In the remaining oil, cook the garlic and dried chillies until fragrant. Watch carefully that the garlic does not burn or else the gravy will taste bitter. Return the chicken and the fried onions back to the pan along with the water.

Cover and leave to simmer for 30-45 minutes, stirring occasionally, until the meat is completely tender. It is ready when the liquid has reduced and the oil has separated from the gravy. Finally check for seasoning before serving.

serves: 4-6
cooking time: 45-60 mins

tip
To make the gravy a little bit more substantial, add 4 fresh or a tin of tomatoes along with the water.

eat with
Green mango salad ... p122
Coconut rice ... p175
Pan-fried tamarind prawns ... p95

chicken masala

ကြက်သားမဆလာ | kyet thar masala

ingredients
¼ teaspoon ground turmeric
1 teaspoon salt
4 thighs and/or drumsticks
100ml peanut oil
1 onion, quartered
3 garlic cloves
2 dried whole chillies, soaked in hot water
½ teaspoon garam masala
½ teaspoon ground coriander
¼ teaspoon ground cumin
150ml water

method
Rub the ground turmeric and salt into the meat, and leave to one side while preparing the onion paste.

Pound the onion, garlic and dried chillies in a pestle and mortar until they resemble a rough paste. Alternatively you can chop everything very finely. Heat the oil in a saucepan and cook the onion paste over moderate heat, stirring occasionally, for 10-15 minutes.

When the onion paste is soft and caramelised, add the spices. Continue to stir until the spices are fragrant. Add the chicken and water, and bring to the boil. Pop the lid on and simmer for 45-60 minutes. Check occasionally to stir or to add more water if necessary. The chicken is ready when it is tender and the oil has separated from the gravy.

serves: 2
cooking time: 55-75 mins

eat with
Red lentil soup ... p183
Golden butter beans ... p119
Panthay noodles ... p153

coconut chicken curry

ကြက်သားအုန်းနို့ဆီပြန် | kyet thar ohn nyot sipyan

A dash of coconut cream added at the end of cooking gives this curry a lovely creamy smoothness. I find the sauce is ideal to eat with noodles or pasta. Just toss the noodles in the sauce and season with a little fish sauce and a generous squeeze of lemon juice.

ingredients
½ teaspoon ground turmeric
½ teaspoon salt
2 tablespoons fish sauce
8 chicken thighs, skinned & boned, cut into 2cm cubes
2 medium onions, quartered
3 garlic cloves
3 dried whole chillies, soaked in hot water
100ml peanut oil
1 tablespoon shrimp paste
1 lemon grass stalk, crushed
4 large tomatoes, chopped
2 tablespoons coconut cream
150ml water
small handful of fresh coriander, chopped

method
Put the ground turmeric, salt and fish sauce in a bowl. Add the chicken and stir to coat with the marinade. Leave for 30 minutes while you make the onion paste.

Using a pestle and mortar, pound the onions, garlic and dried chillies to form a coarse paste or chop everything very finely. Heat the oil in a saucepan and cook the onion paste over a moderate heat for 15-20 minutes until caramelised. Keep moving the paste in the pan so it does not burn. Add the shrimp paste and stir through the mixture.

Put the chicken, lemon grass, tomatoes and water in the pan. Bring to the boil then reduce the heat. Simmer for 25-35 minutes or until the sauce has reduced and the chicken is tender. Add the coconut cream and leave to simmer a further 5 minutes. Sprinkle with coriander just before serving.

serves: 4
cooking time: 45-60 mins

eat with
Coconut rice ... p175
Pickled cucumber ... p212
Sour white radish soup ... p187

chicken with gourd

ကြက်သားဘူးသီးဟင်း | kyet thar budhi hin

ingredients

1 whole chicken, jointed into 8 pieces, or 8 thighs and/or drumsticks
200g gourd, peeled, deseeded and cut into 1cm slices
1 onion, finely chopped
3 garlic cloves, chopped
4 tablespoons peanut oil
½ teaspoon paprika
½ teaspoon ground turmeric
1 teaspoon dried shrimps
2 lemon grass stalks, bruised
1 tablespoon fish sauce
350ml water

method

Heat the oil in a saucepan and cook the onion and garlic for 5-10 minutes. When the mixture is soft and transparent, add the paprika, ground turmeric and dried shrimps. Stir the mixture until the dried shrimps are fragrant, about a minute.

Add the chicken, lemon grass, fish sauce and water. Bring to the boil, cover and simmer for 30-45 minutes. When the meat is tender, add the gourd and continue to simmer over moderate heat for 5-10 minutes or until the gourd is just cooked. Taste and season with a little salt if necessary and serve with rice.

serves: 4
cooking time: 40-65 mins

tip

If gourd is unavailable, use either marrow or courgette and reduce cooking time to 5 minutes.

variations

If you prefer a spicier version, add a few small green chillies.

eat with

Winged bean salad ... p116
Stuffed eggplant ... p106
Red lentil soup .. p183

slow-cooked chicken & potato

ကြက်သားအာလူးဟင်း | kyet thar aloo hin

This is a throw-it-all-in-the-pot dish that requires hardly any work and is perfect for a slow cooker. To do it real justice, use organic chicken and potatoes. It does make a difference because this dish relies solely on the chicken's natural juices to make the gravy tasty.

ingredients
4 chicken pieces, thighs and/or drumsticks
4 small waxy potatoes, peeled and cut into halves
4 large shallots, cut into quarters
6 tablespoons light soy sauce
350ml water
½ teaspoon fresh ground black pepper

method
Put all the ingredients in a saucepan and bring to the boil. Reduce the heat, cover and simmer for 45-60 minutes until the chicken is tender, the potatoes are cooked and the shallots are falling apart. The liquid should have reduced to a thin gravy. Check for seasoning and serve with rice and some stir-fried vegetables.

serves: 2
cooking time: 45-60mins

eat with
Stir-fried & steamed vegetables ... p128
Lotus root & pork rib soup ... p193
Roasted eggplant salad ... p111

egg curry
ဘဲဥဆီပြန် | beh u sipyan

Frying the boiled eggs adds to the flavour and texture of this Indian-inspired curry. We use duck eggs which are richer but hen or even quail eggs work equally well.

ingredients
3 duck eggs, hard-boiled
120ml peanut oil
1 medium onion, quartered
1 garlic clove
1cm fresh ginger
¼ teaspoon ground turmeric
½ teaspoon chilli powder
½ teaspoon garam masala
1 bay leaf
3 large tomatoes, chopped (or 1 tin tomatoes)
1 tablespoon tomato purée
100ml water
1 tablespoon fish sauce
small handful of fresh coriander, chopped

method
Peel the hard-boiled eggs. Make sure they are completely dry by patting them with kitchen paper. Heat 2 tablespoons of oil in a frying pan, preferably non-stick, and fry the hard-boiled eggs. Rotate them gently until they are lightly golden all over. Remove and drain on kitchen paper.

Using a pestle and mortar, pound the onion, garlic and ginger until they resemble a rough paste. Heat the remaining oil in a saucepan. Add the onion paste and cook over a moderate heat for 5-10 minutes until soft and transparent, stirring regularly. Mix in the spices, tomatoes, tomato purée, water and fish sauce. Bring to the boil and simmer for 25-30 minutes until the liquid has reduced and the oil has separated from the sauce.

Cut the eggs vertically in half and gently drop them into the tomato sauce. Wait for a minute or so and turn off the heat. Sprinkle with coriander and serve with basmati rice.

serves: 2
cooking time: 35-45 mins

eat with
Stuffed eggplant ... p106
Pan-fried tamarind prawns ... p95
Red lentil soup ... p183

slow-cooked duck & potato curry

ဘဲသားအာလူးဆီပြန် | beh thar aloo sipyan

The slow-cooking of the onion, garlic and chilli paste give this curry a distinct flavour. Duck and potato are my favourite combination but it works equally well with chicken or just vegetables.

ingredients

¼ teaspoon ground turmeric
¼ teaspoon salt
1 tablespoon fish sauce
½ medium-sized duck, cut into 3cm chunks
4 small waxy potatoes, peeled & cut into halves
1 large onion, quartered
4 garlic cloves, crushed
3 whole dried chillies, soaked in hot water
½ teaspoon paprika
125ml peanut oil
150ml water

method

Put the ground turmeric, salt and fish sauce in a bowl. Add the duck and toss in the marinade. Leave covered in the fridge for 30 minutes.

Make the onion paste. Put the onion, garlic and dried chillies in a pestle and mortar. Pound to a coarse paste. It definitely makes a difference to the taste of the gravy if you use a pestle and mortar. If you don't have one, just chop everything finely.

In a wok or saucepan, heat the oil. First fry the potatoes over high heat, turning regularly, for 2-3 minutes until they are just taking on colour. Remove from the oil and leave to one side. Next add the duck to the oil and let the meat brown slightly all over. Again remove from the oil and set aside.

In the remaining oil, cook the onion paste over moderate heat for 15-20 minutes. It may seem like a lot of oil but it's important not to skimp here. If there is not enough oil, it will burn the onions and make the gravy bitter. Keep a close eye and stir frequently. When the mixture has caramelised and turned reddish brown, add the paprika and stir until fragrant.

Return the potatoes and the duck to the pan, give it a quick stir then add the water. Cover and simmer for 45-60 minutes, occasionally stirring the mixture until the meat is tender. It is ready when the liquid has reduced and the oil has separated from the gravy.

serves: 2
cooking time: 60-85 mins

tip
If you find the amount of oil in this dish too daunting, just spoon some off before serving.

eat with
Water spinach with roasted peanuts ... p112
Lemon relish ... p198
Clear gourd soup ... p184

tamarind duck

မန်ကျည်းဘဲသားဟင်း | magyi beh thar hin

ingredients
½ medium-sized duck, jointed into 4 pieces
6 tablespoons peanut oil
1 onion, quartered
2 garlic cloves
3 whole dried chillies, soaked in hot water
½ teaspoon ground turmeric
25g tamarind pulp
150ml hot water
1 lemon grass stalk, bruised
150ml water

method
Prepare the tamarind. Put the tamarind pulp in a small bowl and pour in the hot water. Leave for a few minutes before mashing up the pulp with a fork. Pour the mixture through a sieve and discard any fibres or stones.

Pound the onion, garlic and chillies in a pestle and mortar or chop everything very finely. Heat the oil in a saucepan and cook the onion paste for 10-15 minutes. When the onion paste is soft and caramelised, add the turmeric and the duck pieces. Stir over moderate heat for a minute or so.

Finally add the tamarind liquid, lemon grass and water. Continue to simmer for 40-50 minutes until the duck is tender and the gravy has reduced. Season with a little salt.

serves: 2
cooking time: 50-65 mins

eat with
Winged bean salad ... p116
Stir-fried prawns & chayote ... p89
Clear gourd soup ... p184

Bagan

This photograph is a reminder of our visit to Ananda Pagoda in Bagan. We spent an afternoon sitting quietly on the cool tiled floor, attempting to blend in with the locals. A number of novice monks stood motionless in meditation, while worshippers went about their daily routine. As we tried to capture the serene faces of the monks, I caught a whiff of a familiar fragrance.

The smell of the yellow champaca flowers stirred long-forgotten memories of my childhood; happy memories that made me feel warm and tingly inside. I was communicating this feeling to Christopher, possibly a little too loudly and the next thing I knew, the lady who was holding a bunch of these yellow flowers came back and gave me some with a knowing smile. I was deeply touched by her kindness and thanked her, forgetting to speak in Burmese!

slow-cooked pork belly

ဝက်သားပဲငံပြာရည် | wet thar pe ngan pya yae

We always talk about my grandmother's slow-cooked pork belly; succulent chunks of meat, flavoured simply by the caramelised sugar and soy sauce. Her secret was her earthenware pot. Used over many years, it had slowly soaked up the oil and juices of previous cooking, until the aroma from the pot itself enhanced the flavour of the pork.

ingredients
2 teaspoons sugar
5 fresh ginger slices
300g pork belly (with fat & skin), cut into large chunks
3 tablespoons light soy sauce
1 tablespoon dark soy sauce
1 tablespoon peanut oil
150ml water

method
Put the sugar, ginger and 1 tablespoon of light soy sauce in a bowl. Mix in the pork and leave to marinate for 30 minutes. Set the oven at 150°C/300°F/Gas2.

Heat the oil in an earthenware pot or a casserole dish. Drop in the pork and any marinade left in the bowl. Let the meat sizzle over moderately high heat until the sugar on the pork has caramelised and any liquid that has come out of the meat has disappeared. Add the dark soy sauce, water and remaining light soy sauce.

Cover with a lid and transfer to the oven, setting the timer for 2 hours. Check the meat, it's ready when it is tender and falls apart easily.

serves: 2, generously
cooking time: 2 hours

tip
Making this the day before and reheating improves the flavour.

eat with
Lemon relish ... p198
Cauliflower & coriander ... p103
Sour white radish soup ... p187

tamarind pork

မန်ကျည်းဝက်သားဟင်း | magyi wet thar hin

This is my favourite pork dish, robust in flavour and the meat melts in the mouth. I usually cook a large pot of this in the hope that it could be eaten over a few days, as the repeated reheating improves the flavour. However in our house, it rarely lasts more than two servings!

ingredients
50g tamarind pulp
250ml hot water
2 large onions, quartered
4 garlic cloves, crushed
3 whole dried chillies, soaked in hot water
120ml peanut oil
¼ teaspoon ground turmeric
1 tablespoon shrimp paste
700g pork, cut into 3cm chunks

method
Prepare the tamarind first. Add the hot water to the tamarind and soak for a few minutes. Use a fork to mash up the pulp and strain through a sieve to remove any fibres or stones.

Using a pestle and mortar, pound the onions, garlic and dried chillies until they resemble a rough paste. Heat the oil in a saucepan and cook the onion paste for 15-20 minutes. When it has caramelised and turned reddish brown, add the turmeric and shrimp paste. Use a wooden spoon to break up the shrimp paste and stir through the mixture.

Add the pork and cook over a moderate heat until any liquid that has come out of the pork has evaporated. Keep stirring to avoid burning the onions. Pour in the tamarind liquid and bring to the boil. Reduce the heat, cover and simmer for 45-60 minutes. Check at regular intervals to make sure the gravy has not dried out. Add a little more water if necessary. Check the pork, it should fall apart easily. Season with a little salt if you wish.

serves: 4
cooking time: 60-80 mins

tip
I recommend making this a day beforehand to allow the pork to absorb all the flavours and become really tender. The next day, reheat and it will taste even better!

eat with
Green mango salad ... p122
Cellophane noodle soup ... p190
Curried bamboo shoots ... p107

pork with green mango
ဝက်သား:သရက်သီး:ဟင်: | wet thar thayet dhi hin

There is a well-known Burmese saying: 'the best meat is pork, the best fruit is mango and the best leaf is tea'. So what could be better than combining two of the best. The tartness of the mango cuts through the richness of the pork, making it beautifully tender.

ingredients
300g boneless pork, cut into 3cm chunks
1 onion, quartered
2 garlic cloves
3 dried whole chillies, soaked in hot water
6 tablespoons peanut oil
¼ teaspoon ground turmeric
1 teaspoon shrimp paste
1 medium unripe green mango, grated with skin on
250ml water

method
Pound the onion, garlic and dried chillies in a pestle and mortar or chop everything very finely. Heat the oil in a saucepan and cook the onion paste over moderate heat. Stir the paste regularly. After 10-15 minutes it should be caramelised and reddish brown. Add the turmeric and shrimp paste. Use a wooden spoon to break up the shrimp paste and stir through the mixture.

Add the pork to the pan, along with the grated mango and water. Bring to the boil, cover and simmer gently for an hour. Remember to stir regularly until the pork is tender and the liquid has reduced to a rich brown sauce. Check for seasoning before serving.

serves: 2
cooking time: 75-80 mins

tip
If you cannot find green mango, you can substitute a bramley apple which will also give the dish its sour fruitiness.

eat with
Tomato fish curry ... p80
Shan tofu salad ... p127
Water spinach with roasted peanuts ... p112

braised pork
ဝက်သားပေါင်း | wet thar baung

This is something I cook when I'm feeling lazy. There's no need to pound onions or wait for them to caramelise. For such little effort, the pork is wonderfully flavourful. A perfect dinner paired with simple fried vegetables.

ingredients
700g pork fillet or tenderloin
600ml water
25g tamarind pulp
50ml hot water
1 tablespoon palm sugar or brown sugar
2 tablespoons fish sauce
1 teaspoon salt

method
Cut the pork into 3cm cubes. Pour the water into a saucepan and drop the meat in. Bring to the boil, cover and simmer for 50-60 minutes until the water has reduced to a third, stirring at regular intervals so the meat doesn't burn.

In a small bowl, soak the tamarind pulp in hot water for a few minutes. Mash the pulp with a fork and strain through a sieve. Pour the tamarind liquid into the pan. Give it a quick stir and add sugar, fish sauce and salt. Continue to simmer gently for a further 15-20 minutes until most of the liquid has disappeared, leaving a tasty gravy.

serves: 4
cooking time: 65-80 mins

eat with
Stir-fried & steamed vegetables ... p128
Clear gourd soup ... p184
Steamed fish in banana leaf ... p84

pork ribs & gourd

ဝက်နံရိုးဘူးသီးဟင်း | wetnanyo budhi hin

ingredients
450g pork ribs
200g gourd or marrow
4 tablespoons peanut oil
1 onion, quartered
2 garlic cloves
3 whole dried chillies, soaked in hot water
½ teaspoon ground turmeric
2 tablespoons fish sauce
250ml water

method
Using a sharp heavy cleaver, cut the ribs into 5cm lengths. Alternatively have your butcher separate the ribs and cut them for you. Peel the gourd, remove the seeds and cut into 1cm slices.

Pound the onion, garlic and chillies in a pestle and mortar to form a coarse paste. Heat the oil in a large saucepan and cook the paste for 5-10 minutes. When it's soft and transparent, stir in the turmeric.

Add the ribs and cook for a few minutes until they are well coated with the onion paste. Mix in water and fish sauce, then bring to the boil. Cover and simmer for about an hour or until the ribs are tender.

If the pan becomes dry, add some more hot water and stir at regular intervals. Finally add the gourd and continue to simmer for 3-4 minutes until the gourd is just cooked. Check for seasoning before serving.

serves: 4
cooking time: 65-75 mins

eat with
Pan-fried tamarind prawns ... p95
Curried bamboo shoots ... p107
Stir-fried & steamed vegetables ... p128

minced pork & salted egg

ဘဲဥဝက်သားပေါင်း | beh u wet thar baung

This is the kind of dish I tend to cook during the winter months. It takes me right back to my childhood, watching my Aunt mincing the pork patiently by hand. For a satisfyingly meaty texture, I also mince the pork coarsely although you can use minced pork from the supermarket.

ingredients

500g lean pork, minced
2 garlic cloves, crushed and chopped
2 tablespoons cornflour
2 tablespoons light soy sauce
½ teaspoon ground black pepper
2 tablespoons preserved cabbage (Dong Cai)
1 egg, beaten
3 salted egg yolks (page 209)

method

Preheat the oven to 180°C/350°F/Gas 4.

Put all the ingredients, except for the salted egg yolks, in a bowl. Use your hands to mix the meat thoroughly. Transfer to an oven-proof dish and spread the mixture so it is 4-5cm thick. Level the mixture with the back of a spoon and place the egg yolks on top, gently pressing them into the meat.

Place the dish in a deep roasting tin and pour hot water into the roasting tin until it comes halfway up the side of the dish. Transfer to the oven and bake for 30 minutes until the pork is cooked through.

serves: 4
cooking time: 30 mins

tip

I find this dish works particularly well eaten with a mixture of chilli sauce, crushed garlic and lemon juice.

eat with

Slow-cooked chicken & potato ... p51
Cellophane noodle soup ... p190
Water spinach with roasted peanuts ... p112

mutton yoghurt curry

ဆိတ်သားဒိန်ချဉ်ဆီပြန် | hseik thar dane chin sipyan

This is perfect food for a cold winter's evening. Tender, juicy pieces of mutton in a gentle aromatic gravy. It reminds me of hot humid days exploring the Indian quarter in Rangoon, where the heady waft of spices and the colourful display of street food delight the senses.

ingredients

700g hogget or mutton, cut into
   3cm cubes
½ teaspoon ground turmeric
2 teaspoons salt
4 tablespoons peanut oil
1 tablespoon sugar
1 large onion, finely chopped
4 garlic cloves, finely chopped
1cm fresh ginger, finely chopped

1 teaspoon crushed dried chillies
1 teaspoon cumin seeds
1 teaspoon coriander seeds
½ teaspoon mustard seeds
1 cinnamon stick
1 bay leaf
½ teaspoon paprika
400ml water
125ml plain yoghurt

method

Rub the ground turmeric and salt into the meat and leave to stand for 15 minutes. In the meantime prepare the spices. Dry roast the cumin, coriander and mustard seeds in a small pan over a low heat for 1-2 minutes, until they start to smell fragrant. Transfer to a pestle and mortar and grind to a fine powder.

Heat the oil in a saucepan and add the sugar. When it starts to caramelise, add the meat and let it brown slightly. Remove from the oil and leave to one side.

In the same pan, add the onion, garlic, ginger and dried chillies. Cook them over a moderate heat for 10-15 minutes. When the mixture is soft and transparent, add the cinnamon stick, bay leaf, paprika and the ground spices. Stir the mixture and add the water and yoghurt.

Return the meat to the pan and simmer with a lid on for an hour or until the mutton is very tender and the gravy has reduced to a thick sauce. Check for seasoning before serving with boiled basmati rice.

serves: 4
cooking time: 75-85 mins

variations

This recipe works with chicken too.

eat with

Pickled vegetables ... p211
Red lentil soup ... p183
Naan bread ... p20

fish & seafood

Eating crabs

Early one morning during our stay in Rangoon, my cousin, Myint Han, came back from the market with two heavy plastic bags. 'You're in luck,' he told me. 'It was full moon last night so it's time to eat crab!'

Having already eaten a second breakfast that morning with his sister, Khin Khin Lat, the thought of more food made me sink into the cane chair, where I sat underneath the whirring ceiling fan, nursing my full stomach. Christopher on the other hand was curious and followed Myint Han into the kitchen. Though neither Christopher nor Myint Han spoke a common language they were still able to communicate.

After some time, Christopher came back to the sitting room and asked, 'What has full moon got to do with eating crabs?' I was about to reply when I realised I wasn't sure. So we both ventured into the kitchen to see a wok on the coal stove now

steaming with crabs. I asked Myint Han about his full moon remark. He explained that the Burmese believed crabs were at their best at this time of the month, when they came out to feed during a low tide.

The crabs were simply boiled and served with a sharp dip of soy sauce, lime juice, crushed garlic and chopped green chillies. The salty sour combination complimented the sweet succulent meat of the crab. It was the best crab I have ever tasted so there must be some truth to the full moon belief. After two break-fasts, and still only ten o'clock in the morning, I could not eat more than half a crab while Christopher somehow put away nearly two.

'Hsa ba,' please eat, Myint Han encouraged. 'Htut hsa ba,' eat more!

boiled crab

ဂထာန်းဟာင်း | ganan hin

With crab this fresh, I prefer not to mess around with it. Simply boil and accompany with a sharp soy sauce dip. For me the pleasure of this simple meal is the experience of eating it; the time and the effort it takes to smash, crack and prise out small morsels of sweet, succulent meat.

ingredients
5 live crabs, scrubbed clean
salt & plenty of water

method
To kill and cook a crab humanely, turn the crab on its back on a chopping board and with the tip of a sharp knife or a skewer, pierce directly behind the eyes and again at the tip of the cone-shaped flap. If you are buying from your local fishmonger and you are a bit squeamish, like me, ask the fishmonger to do this for you.

Half fill a large saucepan with water and add plenty of salt; I use about 35g of salt for every litre of fresh water. When the water is boiling, drop in the crabs and return to the boil. Cook over a moderate heat for 12-20 minutes, according to size. When the crabs are bright orange, remove with tongs, rinse under cold water and set aside to cool.

Remove the grey gills or 'dead man's fingers' and cut into quarters. Serve with a soy sauce dip and let everyone dig in!

serves: 4
cooking time: 20 mins

tip
When choosing crabs make sure they feel heavy for their size, smell fresh and show signs of life.

eat with
Soy sauce dip ... p201

tomato fish curry
ငါးဆီပြန် | nga sipyan

We were served this fish curry at a local roadside restaurant on the way to the Shan state. I love it when we stumble upon such a find. The tomato sauce with tender pieces of fish and fresh coriander made the lengthy car journey worthwhile. When we came back to Rangoon, I asked my cousin if she knew how to cook the fish curry. We spent a wonderful morning cooking, eating and photographing the dish.

ingredients
½ teaspoon ground turmeric
1 tablespoon fish sauce
2 firm white fish fillets
1 large onion, chopped
4 garlic cloves
3 whole dried chillies, soaked in hot water

6 tablespoons peanut oil
½ teaspoon paprika
5 ripe tomatoes, blanched in hot water,
    peeled and chopped
handful of fresh coriander, chopped

method
Mix the turmeric and fish sauce in a bowl. Coat the fish with the marinade, cover and leave in the fridge for 30 minutes.

Using a pestle and mortar, pound the onion, garlic and chillies to form a coarse paste or chop everything finely. Heat the oil in a saucepan and caramelise the onion paste over a moderate heat for 10-15 minutes. Watch carefully so it doesn't burn as this will make the sauce bitter.

Mix in the paprika and stir until fragrant before adding the tomatoes. Turn the heat down and simmer for 30 minutes until it has reduced to a thick sauce. Drop in the fish including any marinade and continue to simmer for 5 minutes. Carefully turn the fish and cook a further 5 minutes or until the fish is cooked through (cooking time will vary according to the thickness of the fish).

Before serving, taste and add a splash more fish sauce if necessary. Sprinkle chopped coriander and serve with plenty of basmati rice.

serves: 2
cooking time: 55-60 mins

eat with
Braised pork ... p66
Winged bean salad ... p116
Stuffed eggplant ... p106

tamarind fish
မန်ကျည်းငါးဟင်း | magyi nga hin

ingredients
2 white fish fillets
50g green beans, sliced
1cm fresh ginger, grated
¼ teaspoon ground turmeric
2 tablespoons fish sauce
4 tablespoons peanut oil
1 medium onion, chopped
1 garlic clove, chopped
½ teaspoon paprika
½ teaspoon dried crushed chillies
25g tamarind pulp
250ml hot water

method
Cut each fillet into three pieces and pop into a bowl. Add turmeric, ginger and fish sauce, and marinate for 30 minutes. Next prepare the tamarind. Add the hot water to the pulp and soak for a few minutes. Using a fork mash the tamarind and strain through a sieve to remove any fibres or stones.

Heat the oil in a saucepan and cook the onion and garlic for 10 minutes. When they are soft and transparent, mix in the paprika and chillies. Stir in the tamarind liquid and bring to the boil. Simmer for 10-15 minutes until the gravy has reduced by half. Add the fish and green beans. Continue to simmer for 3-5 minutes until the fish is opaque and white. Season with a little salt and pepper.

serves: 2
cooking time: 25-35 mins

eat with
Egg curry ... p52
Water spinach with roasted peanuts ... p112
Clear gourd soup ... p184

steamed fish in banana leaf
ငါးပေါင်းဖက်ထုပ် | nga baung pet thote

This is a simple yet tasty way to cook fish. Enveloped in banana leaves with their distinct aroma, each parcel seals in the juices making the fish beautifully moist and tender.

ingredients
2 skinless white fish fillets, cut into large pieces
¼ teaspoon ground turmeric
½ teaspoon salt
2 garlic cloves
1cm fresh ginger
1 lemon grass stalk, sliced
2 green chillies
1 teaspoon shrimp paste
2 tablespoons rice flour
50ml water
2 shallots, thinly sliced
2 banana leaves (cut to 30cm x 20cm)
2 small bamboo skewers or cocktail sticks

method
Rub the turmeric and salt on the fish and leave to one side while you prepare the marinade. Pound the garlic, ginger, lemon grass and chillies in a pestle and mortar. Work in the shrimp paste and rice flour then gradually mix in the water.

Place the fish in a bowl and pour the marinade over them. Cover and leave in the fridge for an hour. To make the banana leaves soft and pliable, either soak in hot water or steam for a few minutes.

On each banana leaf, place a portion of fish including the marinade and sprinkle with sliced shallots. Fold the bottom third of the leaf over the fish, then fold the sides in and the top down to form a rectangular parcel. Secure the parcel with a bamboo skewer.

Place in a steamer for 8-10 minutes until the fish is cooked through. Serve immediately with coconut rice.

serves: 2
cooking time: 10 mins

tip
If banana leaves are unavailable, you can use foil. Place in a medium preheated oven for 10-15 minutes until the fish is cooked.

eat with
Coconut chicken curry ... p45
Shrimp & cellophane noodle salad ... p141
Pork with green mango ... p65

slow-cooked fish
ငါးသလောက်ပေါင်း | nga thalout baung

This dish I consider to be rather special. The fish is stewed slowly until all the bones are so soft they melt in the mouth. In Burma, we use hilsa which is a bony freshwater fish similar to the American shad. Here in the UK, I look for a similar oily fish, whatever is fresh at the local fishmonger, like herring or sometimes even sardines.

marinade
2 tablespoons white vinegar
half lemon, juiced
1 tablespoon fish sauce
½ teaspoon salt
¼ teaspoon ground turmeric

ingredients
700g hilsa or similar fish
6 tablespoons peanut oil
1 onion, quartered
3 garlic cloves, chopped
3 dried whole chillies, soaked in hot water
2 lemon grass stalks, bruised
2 tomatoes, chopped
2 shallots, sliced
500ml water

method
Wash the fish then remove the fins, tail and head. If you are using a small fish like a sardine, you can cook the fish whole including the head which can be eaten. Otherwise cut the fish into thick steaks, about 6cm wide. With a sharp knife make a few deep scores on both sides of the steak. This is important as it will help the marinade penetrate right through to the bones.

Mix together the marinade ingredients and pour over the fish. Cover with cling film and leave in the fridge for at least a couple of hours or more.

Next, pound the onion, garlic and dried chillies in a pestle and mortar until they resemble a rough paste or chop everything very finely. Heat the oil in a saucepan and caramelise the onion paste over a moderate heat, about 10-15 minutes.

Add the fish including the marinade, lemon grass, tomatoes, sliced shallots and water. Bring to the boil, cover with a tight-fitting lid and simmer over a low heat.

Every half an hour, check the fish to make sure it has not dried up. Add a little more water if necessary. After 2 hours of gentle stewing, test the fish. It is ready when the bones fall apart and the oil has separated from the gravy. Taste and season with a little salt if you wish.

serves: 4
cooking time: 2 hours plus

tip
This works particularly well in a pressure cooker or slow cooker.

eat with
Sour white radish soup ... p187
Green mango salad ... p122
Stir-fried prawns & chayote ... p89

stir-fried prawns & chayote
ပုဇွန်ဂေါ်ရခါးသီး | pazoon gurkha dhi

ingredients
1 small chayote, peeled, deseeded and cut into ½cm slices
200g raw prawns, shelled
1 garlic clove, roughly chopped
1 tablespoon peanut oil
salt & pepper for seasoning

method
Have all the ingredients prepared before you start to cook as everything happens very quickly. Heat the oil in a wok, then when it is very hot add the garlic. Toss the garlic for a few seconds until fragrant but without colouring.

Throw in the chayote and stir fry for 2-3 minutes; keep tossing and moving. Finally add the prawns and continue to toss for 1-2 minutes until the prawns are pink and opaque. Season with a little salt and pepper before serving.

serves: 4
cooking time: 5 mins

tip
Choose a small firm chayote without any blemishes. It should be light to medium green in colour.

eat with
Tamarind pork ... p62
Clear gourd soup ... p184
Roasted eggplant & egg ... p125

golden tiger prawns

ရွှေပုဇွန်ဆီပြန် | shwe pazoon sipyan

Tiger prawns are considered a luxury in Burma and this is a wonderful way to cook them. We use the small drop of yellowish orange oil found in the prawn's head which gives the curry an intense flavour and a vibrant golden colour.

ingredients

450g whole fresh tiger prawns
¼ teaspoon ground turmeric
½ teaspoon salt
1 onion, quartered
2 garlic cloves
1cm fresh ginger
3 whole dried chillies, soaked in hot water
6 tablespoons peanut oil
4 tomatoes, finely chopped
125ml water
1 tablespoon fish sauce
small handful of fresh coriander, chopped

method

Gently pull the head off each prawn and from the base of the head, scoop out the small amount of yellowish orange oil. This is like gold dust so carefully spoon into a bowl. Now remove the shells from the prawns but keep the tails on. Using a sharp knife, make a shallow cut along the length of the back and remove the vein.

Add the turmeric, salt and the prawns to the bowl. Mix with your hands until the prawns are coated with the oil. Cover and leave in the fridge while preparing the sauce.

Using a pestle and mortar, pound the onion, garlic, ginger and dried chillies until a rough paste, or chop everything very finely. Heat the oil in a saucepan and cook the onion paste for 10-15 minutes, stirring frequently.

When the paste has caramelised, mix in the tomatoes and water. Turn up the heat and bring to the boil. Cover and gently simmer for 15-20 minutes until the sauce has reduced. Add the prawns and the marinade and stir into the mixture. The prawns should be cooked after 2-3 minutes. Season with fish sauce and sprinkle with coriander before serving.

serves: 4
cooking time: 30-40 mins

eat with
Burmese stir-fried rice ... p168
Winged bean salad ... p116
Stir-fried & steamed vegetables ... p128

pan-fried tamarind prawns
ပုဇွန်မန့်ကျည်းကြော် | pazoon magyi kyaw

During the monsoon months when the streets in our neighbourhood flood, the inconven-
ience of wading through murky water is soon rewarded with an abundance of prawns
and shrimps at the local market. We all look forward to eating juicy fresh prawns fried
simply with tamarind. This particular recipe always reminds me of those precious days.

ingredients
450g whole fresh tiger prawns
25g tamarind pulp
150ml hot water
2 teaspoons sugar
4 tablespoons peanut oil

method
Put the tamarind in a bowl and add the hot water. Leave to soak for a few minutes
before mashing with a fork. Strain the pulp through a sieve to remove any fibres and
stones. The tamarind liquid should be fairly thick. Mix in the sugar.

Prepare the prawns. Remove just the middle section of the shell and leave the heads
and tails on. Using a sharp knife, make a shallow cut along the exposed back and remove the vein.

Pour the tamarind liquid over the prawns and make sure they are evenly coated. Cover
with cling film and marinate in the fridge for at least 20 minutes.

Heat the oil in a wok, then when it is very hot drop in one prawn at a time. This will help
keep the heat consistent in the wok. When all the prawns are in, add any remaining
tamarind liquid. Leave for a minute before tossing the prawns. They should be pink and
opaque after 2-3 minutes. Season with salt and serve immediately.

serves: 4
cooking time: 10 mins

eat with
Coconut chicken curry ... p45
12 ingredient soup ... p192
Water spinach with roasted peanuts ... p112

vegetables & salads

fresh vegetable spring rolls

ကော်ပြန့် | kaw pyant

This is my family's recipe for kaw pyant (popiah in Chinese), which are essentially fresh spring rolls. This is one of the dishes we cook together as a family, when everyone jostles for space in the kitchen to help slice, chop and shred. My mother insists that each vegetable is cooked separately before they are combined together at the end. Then the fun begins when we all sit down to roll our own kaw pyant.

filling ingredients
350g white cabbage, finely shredded
200g carrots, finely shredded
150g bean sprouts
100g bamboo shoots, cut into
    thin matchsticks
100g green beans, sliced thinly
1 small chayote, peeled, seeded and
    sliced into matchsticks
50g deep-fried tofu, cut into
    thick matchsticks
50g cellophane noodles, cooked in
    boiling water for 2-3 mins
4 tablespoons peanut oil
1½ teaspoons sugar
4 teaspoons salt
1 teaspoon light soy sauce
1 teaspoon dark soy sauce
black pepper to season

black bean sauce
1 tablespoon black bean sauce
4 tablespoons water
1 teaspoon cornflour
2 tablespoons sugar

hot sauce
3 large red chillies
3 garlic cloves
2 lime, juiced
1 teaspoon salt

wrappers
24 popiah skins or spring roll wrappers
    (19cm x 19cm)
1 green lettuce, washed and torn into
    large pieces

method
If you are using frozen spring roll wrappers, remove from the freezer to defrost. Remove from their packaging and cover with a damp cloth so they don't dry out.

In a wok, heat ½ tablespoon of oil and stir fry the white cabbage over a moderate heat. Stir in ¼ teaspoon sugar, tossing frequently for a couple of minutes until just cooked. Turn out into a saucepan, large enough to accommodate all the vegetables.

Repeat this step with the carrots, bean sprouts, bamboo shoots, green beans and chayote, cooking them individually with a little oil and sugar. Once all the vegetables are done, mix them thoroughly and season with salt and pepper.

Lightly fry the tofu in ½ tablespoon of oil and the light soy sauce. Transfer to a small dish. While the wok is still hot, toss the cellophane noodles in the remaining oil and add the dark soy sauce. Once the noodles are coated, transfer to a bowl.

Put all the black bean sauce ingredients in a small saucepan and simmer until the sauce has thickened, about 5-10 minutes. Taste a little, it should be slightly sweet and salty. Add more sugar if necessary then pour into a small bowl.

For the hot sauce, pound the red chillies and garlic in a pestle and mortar. Mix in the lime juice and salt for an instant chilli sauce.

Serve at room temperature. To make a spring roll, take a wrapper and spread some dark sauce and hot sauce. Put a piece of lettuce over the top and pile the vegetable mixture lengthways. Sprinkle a generous spoonful of cellophane noodles and fried tofu. Fold one end of the wrapper over the mixture and roll halfway, then fold the two ends in and complete the roll by folding over the top side.

makes: 24
cooking time: 35-50 mins

tip
These spring rolls are also great fried so any leftover filing can be stored in the fridge. The next day, roll them in the wrappers without the lettuce and shallow fry until crispy and golden all over.

variations
This is a vegetarian version which can be used as a base to add other ingredients — chicken, pork, prawns, crab etc.

cauliflower & coriander

ဂေါ်ဖီပန်းနံနံပင် | gorbe pun nannan pyin

ingredients
300g cauliflower, cut into florets of equal size
1 garlic clove, crushed
1 tablespoon peanut oil
125ml water
1 tablespoon light soy sauce
small handful of fresh coriander, chopped

method
Have all your ingredients ready before cooking. Heat the oil in a wok and toss the garlic for 5-10 seconds, until it just starts to turn golden. Quickly throw in the cauliflower and continue to stir fry for 30 seconds. Keep tossing the cauliflower so it does not colour.

Add the water and soy sauce, cover and simmer for 5-10 minutes over a moderate heat until all the water has disappeared. The cauliflower should be cooked but still have bite. Season with a little salt and sprinkle with coriander before serving.

serves: 2
cooking time: 12 mins

eat with
Tamarind duck ... p57
Cellophane noodle soup ... p190
Roasted eggplant salad ... p111

stuffed eggplant

ခရမ်းသီးအစာ သိပ် | khayan dhi asertate

I was a bit of a fussy eater as a child but these stuffed eggplants, full of sweet smoky dried shrimps and onion filling, converted me into an eggplant lover.

ingredients

3 medium eggplants
6 tablespoons peanut oil
1 onion, quartered
3 garlic cloves
3 dried whole chillies, soaked in
   hot water
¼ teaspoon ground turmeric
1 tablespoon shrimp paste
250ml water
1 tablespoon fish sauce
string to tie the eggplants

stuffing

handful of dried shrimps, soaked in
   hot water
1 onion, roughly chopped
2 garlic cloves

method

Make the stuffing first. Drain the dried shrimps and squeeze hard in your hands to remove any water. Put them in a pestle and mortar, along with the onion and garlic. Pound the mixture into a coarse paste. If you do not have a pestle and mortar, put all the stuffing ingredients in a food processor and blitz in bursts.

Cut each eggplant from just beneath the stem all the way down its length. Then slice again lengthways so that it is cut into quarters and still held together by the stem. With a small knife, hollow out some of the flesh from each quarter. Chop this up into small pieces and put to one side for later use.

Divide the stuffing into three portions. Take an eggplant in one hand and push the two quarters together to form a hollow. Spoon in the stuffing and press down the other half so it is a whole again. With a sharp knife score the skin on each quarter. Thread a piece of string around the scores on the eggplant and secure with a knot. This will help keep the stuffing inside.

Next pound the onion, garlic and dried chillies in a pestle and mortar into a coarse paste or chop everything finely. Find a saucepan that can accommodate the eggplants so they do not have to be stacked. Heat the oil in the pan and caramelise the onion paste. Stir in the turmeric and shrimp paste until incorporated. Add the hollowed-out flesh and the stuffed eggplants.

Finally add water and fish sauce, then bring to the boil. Cover and simmer for 30-45 minutes. When the eggplants are soft and the sauce has reduced, check for seasoning. Remove the string before serving.

serves: 4
cooking time: 45-60 mins

eat with
Tamarind fish ... p83
Cauliflower & coriander ... p103
Minced pork & salted egg ... p70

curried bamboo shoots

မျှစ်ဆီပြန် | myit sipyan

Fresh locally grown bamboo shoots have a fantastic flavour and a firm texture. If you do find fresh bamboo shoots, they need to be peeled and boiled for 20 minutes before being used in this recipe. You can also use canned bamboo shoots from an Asian supermarket.

ingredients
1 onion, finely chopped
3 garlic cloves, finely chopped
1cm fresh ginger, peeled and grated
6 tablespoons peanut oil
¼ teaspoon ground turmeric
¼ teaspoon paprika
5 small green chillies
3 tomatoes, chopped
handful of dried shrimps, soaked in hot water
270g bamboo shoots, sliced
200ml water
1 tablespoon fish sauce

method
Heat the oil in a saucepan and cook the onion, garlic, and ginger over a moderate heat for 5-10 minutes. When they are soft and transparent, stir in the turmeric, paprika and dried shrimps. Let the shrimps cook a little until they are fragrant.

Add the green chillies, chopped tomatoes, bamboo shoots and water. Bring to the boil, cover and simmer for 15-20 minutes. When the liquid has reduced and the oil has separated from the gravy, season with fish sauce and serve with rice.

serves: 4
cooking time: 20-30 mins

eat with
Slow-cooked pork belly ... p61
Stir-fried & steamed vegetables ... p128
Lotus root & pork rib soup ... p193

roasted eggplant salad

ခရမ်းသီးဖုတ်သုတ် | khayan dhi pope thote

This salad is wonderfully intense, not only from the aromatic crispy garlic and fresh co-riander, but also because the roasted eggplants give it a distinctive smoky flavour. The chopped peanuts and sesame seeds add a crunchy texture to the soft flesh, which is dressed with garlic oil, fish sauce and lime juice.

ingredients
2 medium eggplants
2 small shallots, thinly sliced & soaked in cold water
2 garlic cloves, thinly sliced
2 tablespoons peanut oil

garnishes
1 teaspoon dried shrimps, pounded into floss
1 teaspoon toasted sesame seeds
1 teaspoon roasted peanuts, chopped
small handful of fresh coriander, chopped
½ lime, juiced
1 tablespoon fish sauce

method
To get that lovely smoky flavour, place the eggplants whole on a flat baking sheet lined with foil. Pierce the eggplants with a knife to stop them bursting during cooking. Place under a hot grill for 15-25 minutes turning them occasionally. Be sure to let the skin colour and char. While the eggplants are grilling, make the crispy garlic and oil. Heat the oil in a small saucepan and fry the garlic until golden and aromatic. Remove with a slot-ted spoon and cool. Drain the shallots and squeeze them in your hands to remove any water. Pop them in a bowl.

When the eggplants are ready, cool a little until they can be handled. Cut them in half and scoop out the flesh into the bowl. Mix in 1 tablespoon of the frying oil and the gar-nishes. Taste and adjust the seasoning so there is a balance of salt and sourness. Serve while the salad is still a little warm.

serves: 2
cooking time: 25 mins

tip
For vegetarians, you can substitute the dried shrimps and fish sauce with either soy sauce or a pinch of salt.

eat with
Tomato fish curry ... p80
Braised pork ... p66
Sour white radish soup ... p187

water spinach with roasted peanuts
ကန်စွန်းရွက်ကြော် | kasun ywet kyaw

ingredients
1 tablespoon peanut oil
1 garlic clove, roughly chopped
250g water spinach
1 tablespoon rice wine or dry sherry
15g roasted peanuts, roughly chopped
½ small onion, thinly sliced

method
As with all stir-fry dishes, have all the ingredients prepared as the cooking takes very lit-tle time. Wash the water spinach carefully - sometimes the hollow stems hide a few bits of grit. Pluck the leaves and cut the stems into short lengths.

To take the edge off the onions, soak them in cold water for a few minutes. Drain and squeeze out any water with your hands.

Heat the oil in a wok and fry the garlic for a few seconds until fragrant. Throw in the stems first and continue to stir fry for a minute, then add the leaves. Keep tossing and moving the contents in the wok.

Pour in the rice wine and stir until it has evaporated. Season with salt and sprinkle with roasted chopped peanuts and sliced onions on top.

serves: 4
cooking time: 5 mins

tip
If water spinach is unavailable, use other leafy greens.

eat with
Slow-cooked fish ... p88
Roasted eggplant salad ... p111
Dried shrimp relish ... p200

roselle leaves & bamboo curry

ချဉ်ပေါင်ရွက်ကြော် | chin baung kyaw

I am very fond of roselle leaves possibly because they were the only greens I ate without any persuasion when I was a child. Cooked in this way, they make a spicy, sour and salty concoction. A bowl of chin baung kyaw, rice and ngapi kyaw (dried shrimp relish) was my idea of a perfect meal.

ingredients
400g roselle leaves
100ml peanut oil
2 medium onions, quartered
4 garlic cloves, chopped
3 whole dried chillies, soaked in hot water
¼ teaspoon ground turmeric
2 tablespoons dried shrimps
100g canned bamboo shoots, sliced
5 small green chillies
100ml water
fish sauce to taste

method
Pluck the roselle leaves. Discard the stems and wash the leaves thoroughly then drain. Pound the onions, garlic and dried chillies into a coarse paste in a pestle and mortar or chop everything very finely.

Heat the oil in a saucepan and cook the onion paste over moderate heat, stirring frequently, for 10-15 minutes. When it is soft and caramelised, add the turmeric and dried shrimps. Stir for a minute until the shrimps are fragrant.

Add the roselle leaves and stir with a wooden spoon until the leaves have wilted. Mix in the bamboo shoots, green chillies and water. Cover and simmer for 15-20 minutes until the leaves have turned dark green and the liquid has reduced. Season with fish sauce and taste. There should be a good balance of sourness, salt and spiciness.

serves: 4
cooking time: 25-35 mins

tip
When roselle leaves are unavailable, you can use spinach but you will need to add the juice of half a lemon to create the tangy flavour.

eat with
Slow-cooked duck & potato curry ... p56
Cellophane noodle soup ... p190
Dried shrimp relish ... p200

winged bean salad

ပဲစောင်းရားသုတ် | pe saun yah thote

Winged beans, also known as four-angled or goa beans, are lovely when eaten raw in a salad. The pods are juicy and crunchy when they are young. Choose ones that are about 10-12cm long. The more mature pods can be a little bitter and require blanching in hot water first.

for crispy shallots & oil
2 shallots, thinly sliced lengthways
peanut oil

ingredients
100g winged beans
1 tablespoon fish sauce
1 lime, juiced
1 tablespoon dried shrimps, pounded into floss
1 teaspoon roasted sesame seeds
1 teaspoon dried chilli flakes

method
Make the crispy shallots first. Pour the oil into a small saucepan to about a third of the way up. When the oil is hot, fry the shallots until golden. Remove from the oil and set aside. Reserve 1 tablespoon of the frying oil for the salad dressing.

If the beans are mature pods, blanch them in salted boiling water for no more than a minute or two. They should still have bite. Tip them into a bowl of cold water to stop the cooking process and then drain. Slice the beans thinly on a slight diagonal.

Just before serving, assemble the salad. Put the remaining ingredients in a bowl including the frying oil and half the crispy shallots. Toss the beans in the salad dressing and check for seasoning. Finally sprinkle with the remaining crispy shallots.

serves: 2
cooking time: 10-15 mins

variations
When winged beans are not available, substitute with green beans or bean sprouts. Slice the green beans similarly but keep the bean sprouts whole.

eat with
Red lentil soup ... p183
Golden tiger prawns ... p92
Steamed fish in banana leaf ... p84

golden butter beans

ရွှေ‌ရောင်ပဲဟင်း | shwe yaung pe hin

Butter beans are also known as Lima, Calico, Madagascar or Snow beans. These large white beans have a rich and creamy texture that helps them to soak up the turmeric and onion flavours, turning them deep yellow. I think this is typical of Burmese cooking, simple but full of flavour.

ingredients
200g dried butter beans, soaked overnight
4 tablespoons peanut oil
½ onion, thinly sliced lengthways
¼ teaspoon ground turmeric
300ml water

method
Heat the oil in a saucepan and fry the onion over medium heat. Be sure to stir frequently so it cooks evenly and does not burn. As soon as it is turning golden, add the turmeric and stir the mixture for a few seconds. Remove from the oil and set aside.

Add the butter beans and water to the pan, then bring to the boil. Continue to boil rapidly for 10 minutes then reduce the heat and cover with a lid. Simmer for 30 minutes or until the water has been absorbed completely. The beans should be tender; if not add a little more water and cook until soft. Season with salt and sprinkle with the fried onions.

serves: 4
cooking time: 45 mins

tip
For a quick version, use canned beans that are already cooked. Just omit the water and cook in the turmeric oil for a few minutes until the beans are tender and infused with flavour.

variations
This recipe also works well with chickpeas or yellow spit peas. For additional colour and spice, add dried chilli flakes or paprika.

eat with
Coconut rice ... p175
Sour white radish soup ... p187
Green mango salad ... p122

green mango salad
သရက်သီးသုတ် | thayet dhi thote

The Burmese version of green mango salad uses cooked shallot oil to flavour the tangy spicy salad. Choose a firm, unripe green mango so it has a natural fruity sourness.

for crispy shallots & oil
1 shallot, sliced lengthways
peanut oil

ingredients
1 small green mango, peeled
1 shallot, thinly sliced
2 green chillies, sliced
1 tablespoon fish sauce
1 tablespoon dried shrimps, pounded into floss
1 teaspoon roasted chickpea powder (page 208)
1 teaspoon toasted sesame seeds
fresh coriander leaves for decoration

method
Pour the oil into a small saucepan to about a third of the way up. Heat the oil and fry the shallots until golden. Remove from the oil and set aside. Reserve 1 tablespoon of the frying oil for the salad dressing. Then prepare all the other salad ingredients prior to shredding the mango.

In Burma there is a special way of cutting mango called 'pauk'. They hold the mango firmly in one hand, then strike it with a sharp knife, cutting thin shreds of the flesh. I prefer to use a grater or chop the mango into matchsticks, discarding the stone. Place the mango in some kitchen paper and squeeze to remove any liquid from it.

Put all the ingredients in a bowl including 1 tablespoon of frying oil and half the crispy shallots. Toss the salad, check for seasoning and sprinkle with the remaining crispy shallots before serving.

serves: 2
cooking time: 10-15 mins

tip
You can also use green papaya for this salad. If neither mango or papaya is available, I use a kohlrabi. It has a similar texture albeit a little more juicy when shredded. However it's not naturally tart so you will need to add a little lemon or lime juice.

eat with
Burmese stir-fried rice ... p168
Stuffed eggplant ... p106
Minced pork & salted egg ... p70

roasted eggplant & egg
ခရမ်းသီးဖုတ်ကြက်ဥ | khayan dhi pope ceku

A quick and easy way to prepare eggplants. The char-grilling gives the eggplant a lovely smokiness and the egg gives it an extra depth of richness.

ingredients
2 small eggplants
2 tablespoons peanut oil
2 small shallots, thinly sliced lengthways
1 egg, beaten
1 tablespoon fish sauce
small handful fresh coriander, chopped

method
To get that smoky flavour, place the eggplants whole on a flat baking sheet lined with foil. Pierce with a knife to stop them bursting during cooking. Place under a hot grill for 15-25 minutes, turning occasionally, until the skins are charred and the insides are soft.

Remove the eggplants from the grill and cool until they can be handled. Cut them in half and scoop out the insides. I particularly like the skins too, so I chop these finely and mix them in with the flesh.

To make the crispy shallots, heat the oil in a small saucepan and fry the shallots until golden. Remove from the oil and drain on kitchen paper. Add the chopped eggplants to the pan and warm through over moderate heat.

Add the egg and stir until just scrambled. Season with fish sauce then sprinkle with coriander and crispy shallots before serving.

serves: 2
cooking time: 15-20 mins

tip
Vegetarians can replace the fish sauce with a little salt.

eat with
Chicken with gourd ... p46
Pan-fried tamarind prawns ... p95
Stir-fried & steamed vegetables ... p128

shan tofu salad

ရှမ်းတို့ဟူးသုတ် | shan tohu thote

Shan tofu is made with gram flour and turmeric which gives it a distinct yellow colour. The tofu is straightforward to make. It takes a day to soak and another to set. I usually make a large batch as it will keep in the fridge for a few days. If there are any leftovers, you can cut them into slices, deep fry until crispy and dip in chilli sauce.

for the tofu
200g gram flour (chana dal)
1.9 litres water
¼ teaspoon ground turmeric
1 teaspoon salt
oil to grease saucepan
a piece of muslin cloth or double gauze
2 plastic containers (17cm x 12cm x 5cm)

salad dressing
1 onion, made into crispy onions
  (page 206)
2 tablespoons onion oil (page 206)
2 tablespoons tamarind juice
1 tablespoon roasted chickpea powder
  (page 208)
3 green chillies, sliced
2 tablespoons fish sauce
1 lime, juiced
small handful of fresh coriander, chopped

method
Put the gram flour in a large mixing bowl and slowly pour in the water while whisking to remove any lumps. Cover and leave to soak overnight.

The following day, line a sieve with the muslin cloth and place over a clean bowl. Slowly pour in the soaked flour. Use a wooden spoon to gently help the mixture go through and discard any residue left in the cloth. Leave the liquid to stand.

After an hour, using a ladle remove and discard 900ml of the liquid without disturbing the sediment at the bottom of the bowl.

Grease a large saucepan with a little oil and carefully pour in the remaining liquid. You will find a thick paste of sediment at the bottom which should be kept to one side. This paste is used to thicken the tofu later.

Mix in turmeric and salt, and simmer over a moderate heat for 10-15 minutes, stirring continuously. As the mixture starts to thicken, add a tablespoon of the leftover paste and continue to stir for 5 minutes, until the mixture is the consistency of a thick glossy custard. I like my tofu firm to the touch but still silky soft. If you prefer a firmer tofu, add all the thickening paste.

Remove from the heat and pour into the plastic containers, greased with oil. Leave to cool completely, then cover and transfer to the fridge. The next day, ease the tofu out of the container and cut into 1cm slices. Prepare the salad dressing ingredients and toss gently with the tofu just before serving.

serves: 8
cooking time: 25 mins, not including soaking and resting

eat with
Clear gourd soup ... p184
Egg curry ... p52
Stir-fried prawns & chayote ... p89

stir-fried & steamed vegetables

 | dhi sone kyaw

Here's a simple way to cook vegetables that keep their colour and texture. Use either garlic or ginger to flavour the oil first, or any onion oil that might have accumulated from frying crispy onions.

ingredients
350g seasonal vegetables
1 garlic clove, chopped, or 3 slices of fresh ginger
2 tablespoons peanut oil
2-3 tablespoons water
1 tablespoon light soy sauce

method
Choose 2-3 vegetables that are in season. Dice or slice each vegetable so the pieces are uniform in size, which makes the dish look more pleasing. Keep each vegetable separate as they may cook for different times.

Heat the wok on a high heat for a minute before adding the oil. If you are using a non-stick wok then omit this step.

Drizzle the oil into the wok making sure it coats the sides as well as the bottom. Throw in the garlic or ginger and toss regularly for a few seconds. Add the vegetables according to density. Keep the vegetables moving constantly in the wok for a minute or so.

Add a little water at a time and let it bubble away until evaporated. Add the soy sauce and toss with the vegetables. Season with a little salt and pepper before serving.

serves: 2
cooking time: 5 mins

eat with
Dried shrimp relish ... p200
Spicy bean curd & peanut sauce ... p205

noodles

traditional fish noodle soup

မုန့်ဟင်းခါး | mohingar

When it comes to comfort food, mohingar is top of my list. It brings back fond memories of early morning visits to Shwedagon Pagoda which started with breakfast at a mohingar stall nearby. This noodle soup is considered the Burmese national dish and is eaten for breakfast, lunch and dinner. Not surprisingly every family has their own variation and this is my family's recipe. Nowadays I prefer to eat mohingar nearer lunchtime and invite a group of friends to join in this hearty Burmese brunch.

prepare the fish
300g catfish (or use whole trout)
1 lemon grass stalk, bruised
¼ teaspoon ground turmeric
500ml water

to make the onion paste
1 large onion, chopped
3 cloves garlic
1cm fresh ginger
2 lemon grass stalks, white part only
3 whole dried chillies, soaked in hot water
1 teaspoon shrimp paste
½ teaspoon paprika
½ teaspoon ground turmeric
6 tablespoons peanut oil

to make the soup
1.5 litres water
100g young banana stem, sliced
(alternatively use 12 small
    shallots, peeled)
75g ground rice powder, roasted
3 tablespoons fish sauce
1 teaspoon ground black pepper

eat with
500g fine rice noodles or
    wheat noodles, cooked
3 limes, halved
5 hard-boiled eggs, peeled & quartered
2 handfuls of fresh coriander, chopped
gourd or onion crispy fritters (page 21)
extra fish sauce & chilli flakes

method
Put the fish in a large pan, add the water, lemon grass and turmeric. Bring to the boil and simmer for 6-10 minutes until the fish is just cooked. Remove the fish from the pan and when cool enough to handle, peel the skin and flake the flesh, discarding any bones. Drain the fish stock through a sieve and reserve for the soup.

Pound the onion, garlic, ginger, dried chillies and lemon grass into a paste in a pestle and mortar, otherwise just chop everything as finely as you can.

Heat the oil in a saucepan and add the onion paste. Cook over moderate heat for 15-20 minutes until the paste is soft and caramelised. Add the shrimp paste, mash with a wooden spoon until incorporated, then mix in the turmeric and paprika. Cook for a further minute until the spices are fragrant before adding the flaked fish. Pop the lid on and cook for 10-15 minutes, allowing all the flavours from the onion paste to infuse into the fish.

The soup paste is done. If you are making this in advance, cool the mixture completely and pop in the freezer. It will keep for up to 1 month.

To make the soup: put the soup paste (completely defrosted if using from frozen), rice powder, water and the reserved fish stock (or 500ml of water if not using fish stock) in a large pan. Bring to a boil while stirring continuously to make sure the rice powder doesn't clump. Add the shallots or banana stem and simmer for 20-30 minutes until they are tender. Add the fish sauce and taste for seasoning. Finally add lots of black pepper before serving.

To serve, put a handful of noodles in a bowl and ladle over the soup. Let everyone add the garnishes as they wish. It should taste spicy, salty and tangy from the limes.

serves: 4-6
cooking time: 50-70 mins

flat rice noodles with eggs

 | nyat khaut swe kyaw

ingredients
½ small onion, thinly sliced lengthways
3 tablespoons peanut oil
200g bean sprouts
2 eggs
350g fresh flat rice noodles
1 tablespoon chilli & dried shrimp oil (page 212)
1 tablespoon fish sauce
small handful of fresh coriander

method
When you buy fresh flat rice noodles from an Asian store, they come folded and you will need to pull each noodle apart to separate them. If you are using dried noodles, cook as per packet instructions.

Heat the oil in a wok and fry the sliced onions until golden brown. Remove from the oil and set aside. Next add the bean sprouts and eggs. Stir with a wooden spoon for a minute or so until the eggs are scrambled and the bean sprouts are soft. Mix in the chilli & dried shrimp oil, noodles and fish sauce. Toss the noodles every few seconds until they are well incorporated with the other ingredients. Check for seasoning and sprinkle with crispy onions and chopped coriander.

serves: 2
cooking time: 15 mins

variations
I like this plain version of the flat rice noodles. However chicken, pork or prawns can be added.

eat with
Clear gourd soup ... p184

Shwedagon
pagoda {part 1}

The dazzling golden glow of Shwedagon stupa rising up to illuminate the vast night sky of Rangoon is an unforgettable sight. To me it is a symbol of home.

Visiting the pagoda was a favourite family day out, to make offerings of flowers, candles and prayer flags in honour of Buddha. Encased deep within the shrine, there are said to be eight sacred hairs of Buddha. Pilgrims from all over the country come to pay homage, especially on auspicious religious days and at least once in their lifetime.

The main stupa, plated with gold, towers over 100 metres from its platform. The very top is adorned with thousands of diamonds, rubies, sapphires and other gems. Countless smaller shrines and pavilions crowd around the wide-marbled platform that encircles the main stupa. Despite the number of pilgrims and visitors, the pagoda remains a place of serenity and sublime beauty even to this day.

One of my earliest memories is of a visit to Shwedagon at dawn. On the way, we stopped by our favourite Mohingar stall where regular diners hunched over low stools slurping fish noodle soup and catching up on daily gossip. The stall owner knew our family well. Considered loyal customers, we were offered a second helping of soup. With satisfied stomachs, we returned to the car, turned towards Singuttara Hill and parked at the eastern gate.

We removed our shoes before beginning the long climb up the covered stairway lined with numerous stalls. After walking past the first few stalls we overtook a couple who were waiting for the remainder of their family to join them. 'Come and rest a bit. Leave your shoes here. We have fresh flowers,' voices from other stall owners tried to compete for customers as more people ascended behind us. My father, however, favoured a particular stall where the owner with a betel-stained smile greeted us. For a small fee we left our shoes in his care.

As for the flowers and other offerings, my mother led us nearly all the way up the staircase to a small stall. The owner was a woman with friendly eyes and two enthusiastic young helpers. My mother paused to chat to the woman and gave advice for her chesty cough and invited the woman to visit her

health clinic. The woman offered my mother two large bunches of flowers, a handful of candles and a packet of gold leaf in gratitude but my mother insisted on paying her. My sister and I carried a bunch of flowers each and ran up the remaining steps, trying to beat our two older brothers to the top.

[continued on page 171]

hand-mixed noodle salad

လက်သုတ် | let thote sone

This is a unique dish and as the name suggests you mix the salad with your hands. It's served with all the individual ingredients laid out on the table and the fun of eating this salad is making it yourself; mashing the potatoes, feeling the wonderful textures of the noodles and adjusting the garnishes until there is a perfect balance of all the seasoning. I like mine with a generous squeeze of lime juice so it's deliciously sharp and eat it Burmese style using my fingers.

ingredients
100g basmati rice, cooked
1 teaspoon chilli & dried shrimp oil
    (page 212)
4 large floury potatoes, peeled & cut
    into 1cm slices
100g egg noodles, cooked
    (spaghetti is OK)
100g cellophane noodles, cooked
100g flat rice noodles, cooked
100g rice vermicelli, cooked
150g white cabbage, shredded finely
100g deep-fried tofu
shan tofu, halve the recipe on page 127

garnishes
125ml onion oil (page 206)
1 onion made into crispy onions
    (page 206)
50g roasted chickpea powder (page 208)
20g dried shrimps, pounded into floss
3 limes, quartered
75g tamarind pulp
200ml hot water
large handful of fresh coriander, chopped
extra fish sauce & dried chilli flakes

method
A couple of days beforehand, follow the instructions to make the Shan tofu. On the day, prepare the garnishes first. Make the crispy onions and oil, roasted chickpea powder, pound the dried shrimps into floss, chop the coriander and cut the limes. Add the hot water to the tamarind and leave for a few minutes to soften. Use a fork to mash the pulp and strain through a sieve to remove any stones or fibres.

Next prepare the base ingredients. Cook the rice as you would normally then mix in the chilli & dried shrimp oil. Cook the different types of noodles, following their packet instructions. Boil the potatoes for 7-10 minutes until they are tender, drain and leave to cool. Finally shred the cabbage and slice the fried tofu and Shan tofu into ½cm slices.

When all the ingredients are prepared, pile them individually on plates or in bowls and serve at room temperature. To make the perfect thote, take a small handful of each of the base ingredients. Add a teaspoon of crispy onions, chickpea powder, dried shrimps and coriander. Then a tablespoon of oil, a drizzle of tamarind liquid and a dash of fish sauce. Finally sprinkle chilli flakes and squeeze some lime juice, and mix well. It should be salty, sour and spicy.

serves: 6
cooking time: 60 mins

eat with
Clear gourd soup ... p184

shrimp & cellophane noodle salad

ပဲကြာဇံပုဇွန်သုတ် | pe kyazan pazoon thote

The cellophane noodles are eaten cold in this salad which makes it perfect for summer; it's light and yet filling. As with all salads in Burma, it's tossed in a sour, salty and spicy dressing.

ingredients
100g cellophane noodles
100g shelled shrimps, cooked
2 shallots, thinly sliced lengthways
1 tomato, chopped
20g roasted peanuts, chopped
small handful of fresh coriander, chopped
small handful of fresh mint, chopped

salad dressing
2 garlic cloves, sliced
2 tablespoons peanut oil
2 tablespoons fish sauce
1 lime, juiced
½ teaspoon sugar
2 green chillies, chopped

method
To make the salad dressing, fry the garlic in the oil until golden brown. Remove from the oil and set aside. Let the oil cool before adding the remaining dressing ingredients and mix well.

Next boil the cellophane noodles in hot water for 2-3 minutes until they are soft and translucent. Drain and rinse in cold water to stop the cooking process and leave to cool.

Put all the salad ingredients in a large bowl and add the dressing. Toss until the noodles are coated, check for seasoning and sprinkle the fried garlic before serving.

serves: 4
cooking time: 10-15 mins

tip
To reduce the strong taste of raw shallots, soak them in cold water before mixing in the salad.

variations
You can use either pork or chicken instead of shrimp or leave it out completely if you are a vegetarian.

eat with
Clear gourd soup ... p184

coconut noodle soup

အုန်းနို့ခေါက်ဆွဲ | ohn nyot khaut swe

This is a Burmese version of coconut noodle soup made with chicken. It has just the right balance of coconut milk and chicken curry so it's not too rich or oily. The traditional recipe includes duck's blood which is cooked first, forming a jelly-like consistency, before it is cut into cubes and added to the soup. I have omitted this from the recipe as it's difficult to find and really does not alter the taste of the soup.

for the curry
½ chicken
¼ teaspoon ground turmeric
1 tablespoon fish sauce
2 onions, chopped
4 garlic cloves
3 dried whole chillies, soaked in hot water
100ml peanut oil
½ teaspoon paprika
100ml water

to make the soup
1.5 litres chicken stock (made from
  leftover chicken carcass)
3 tablespoons chickpea powder
50ml water
6 shallots, quartered
1 tablespoon condensed milk (optional)
250ml coconut milk

eat with
500g egg noodles, cooked
1 medium onion, thinly sliced lengthways
4 duck eggs, hard boiled and quartered
handful of fresh coriander, chopped
2 limes, quartered
fried crispy noodles (page 206)
extra fish sauce & chilli flakes

method
Strip the meat off the chicken, cut into small cubes and put into a bowl. Keep the carcass for the stock. Mix in the ground turmeric and fish sauce, and leave to marinate for at least 30 minutes.

In the meantime make the chicken stock. Put the carcass in a large pan and cover with plenty of water. Bring to the boil and skim off any scum that has formed. Cover and simmer gently for 30 minutes.

To make the curry, pound the onions, garlic and dried chillies in a pestle and mortar. If you don't have one, chop everything finely. Heat the oil in a saucepan and cook the onion paste over a moderate heat for 10-15 minutes until caramelised. Stir in the paprika, water and the chicken including the marinade. Cover and simmer for 15-20 minutes, stirring at intervals until the oil has separated from the gravy and the meat is tender.

Heat 1.5 litres of the chicken stock in a large saucepan. Mix the chickpea powder with 50ml of water into a paste and slowly stir into the stock. Add the quartered shallots and condensed milk, and simmer for 20 minutes, stirring frequently. When the shallots are tender, add the coconut milk and a third of the chicken curry to the pan. Continue to simmer for a further 5 minutes. Taste for seasoning, adding a little more fish sauce if you wish.

To serve, put a handful of noodles in a bowl with a generous spoonful of the remaining chicken curry, then ladle the soup until it covers the noodles. Put the garnishes on the table to allow each person to add as desired.

serves: 4-6
cooking time: 80-90 mins

tip
If you cannot find duck eggs, use regular hen's eggs.

night market noodles
ဆီချက်ခေါက်ဆွဲ | si chet khaut swe

The direct translation of this dish is cooked oil noodles, but I tend to associate it with the night market in Rangoon because this was the place where my brother and I often went to eat a bowl of these noodles tossed in garlic oil. It usually came with some shredded meat and a bowl of hot chicken soup sprinkled with spring onions. Nowadays whenever I have leftover roast meat, I rustle up these noodles which go down really well.

ingredients
250g fresh egg noodles
3 garlic cloves, thinly sliced
3 tablespoons peanut oil
1 tablespoon light soy sauce
small handful of spring onions, chopped

eat with
shredded roast duck, chicken or pork
chicken soup

method
Bring a large pan of water to the boil. Add a pinch of salt and blanch the noodles for a couple of minutes until they are soft. Drain and rinse under cold water. If you are using dried egg noodles, follow the packet instructions.

Heat the oil in a wok and fry the garlic until golden. Remove from the oil immediately and drain on kitchen paper. Add the noodles and soy sauce, then toss for a minute until the noodles are warmed through and coated with the garlic oil. Check for seasoning and sprinkle with crispy garlic and spring onions. Serve with shredded meat and a bowl of soup.

serves: 2
cooking time: 10 mins

mandalay noodle salad

မန္တလေးမုန့်တီသုတ် | mandalay mouti thote

While we were visiting Mandalay, this was one of the dishes on my list of 'must eat'. The salad is made using thick round rice noodles, tossed with chicken curry, raw shallots, chickpea powder, crispy onions and small fish balls. I like to make a quick version of mouti thote whenever I have leftover chicken curry and add some fried fish cakes.

ingredients
¼ teaspoon ground turmeric
½ teaspoon salt
1 tablespoon fish sauce
4 chicken thighs, skinned
1 medium onion, quartered
2 garlic cloves, crushed
2 whole dried chillies, soaked in hot water
6 tablespoons peanut oil
100ml water
fish cakes, halve the recipe on page 16
400g thick rice noodles, cooked

garnishes
2 shallots, thinly sliced lengthways
4 teaspoons roasted chickpea powder
   (page 208)
3 limes, cut into wedges
1 spring onion, sliced
onion oil (page 206)
1 onion made into crispy onions
   (page 206)
dried chilli flakes & fish sauce

method
Start with the chicken curry as this can be made in advance. Mix the ground turmeric, salt and fish sauce in a bowl and marinate the chicken for 15 minutes or more. Next make the onion paste. Pound the onion, garlic and dried chillies in a pestle and mortar to form a coarse paste.

Heat the oil in a saucepan and cook the onion paste over moderate heat for 15-20 minutes. When the paste has caramelised, add the chicken and water. Bring to the boil then reduce the heat and simmer for 25-35 minutes until the sauce has reduced and the chicken is tender. I tend to cook the chicken on the bone as I find this adds to the taste of the gravy. Cool the chicken a little and strip the meat off the bone then cut into small cubes.

Next follow the fish cakes recipe and cut into slices. Make the crispy onions and oil, reserving some of the frying oil in a small bowl. Prepare the remaining garnishes and cook the rice noodles as per packet instructions. To serve put a large handful of noodles in a bowl with a generous ladle of chicken curry. Let everyone add the garnishes to suit their taste.

serves: 4
cooking time: 45-60 mins, not including fish cakes

tip
If thick rice noodles are unavailable, substitute fresh udon noodles.

eat with
Clear gourd soup ... p184

shwedaung salad

ရွှေတောင်သုပ် | shwedaung thote

At the top of our road in Rangoon, I remember a street stall that sold the best Shwedaung thote. It was a real treat to stroll up there with my cousins and sit by the roadside to slurp down a bowl of these noodles. Every time I try to recreate this dish it reminds me of those precious days. I think it's a great way to eat noodles, the freshness of the lime cuts through the richness of the creamy curry while the shredded cabbage and fried crispy noodles add a wonderful texture and crunch to the salad.

ingredients
coconut chicken curry, halve the recipe on page 45
400g egg noodles, cooked

garnishes
2 small shallots, thinly sliced lengthways
4 teaspoons roasted chickpea powder (page 208)
2 limes, cut into wedges
25g white cabbage, shredded thinly
large handful of vermicelli or rice noodles
150ml peanut oil
handful of fresh coriander, chopped
dried chilli flakes & fish sauce

method
Start with the coconut chicken curry as this can be made in advance. If you are using leftover curry, reheat it making sure it is piping hot all the way through. Add a little water if necessary.

Prepare the garnishes. To make the fried crispy noodles, heat the oil in a small saucepan and add a small amount of vermicelli at a time. The vermicelli will turn white and puff up. Remove immediately with a slotted spoon and drain on kitchen paper.

To serve, put a large handful of noodles on a plate with a ladle of coconut chicken curry. Place the garnishes on the table to allow each person to dress the salad as they wish. The salad should be eaten at room temperature and should taste slightly salty and sour.

serves: 4
Cooking time: 20 mins, not including chicken curry

tip
Soak the shallots in cold water for a few minutes to take away the strong taste.

eat with
Sour white radish soup ... p187

Shan noodles

After a day in the back of a car, travelling along bumpy roads with hardly any loo-stops, we arrived at Nyaung Shwe, a town at the edge of Inle Lake. This fresh water lake is in Shan State, a place my mother remembers fondly. Before I was born, she lived in the Shan hills with my father for a couple of years before returning to Rangoon.

Inle Lake is on most tourist circuits, known for the water villages where Intha people live in houses built on stilts and fisherman have a unique way of rowing a boat with one leg. After a day of sightseeing, my focus was back on food and on top of my list was Shan noodles.

The following morning, we walked around the small town looking for a place to eat Shan noodles for breakfast. As with most places in Burma, there were no obvious signs to indicate a restaurant let alone what they served. It required local knowledge. We stopped by many shops to ask and each person directed us to the same street off the main road.

We followed the directions and found the nondescript store, which we would have mistaken for an ordinary

house, if not for the steaming pot of soup on a charcoal stove and a crowd of people inside. We found two empty seats next to a group of local women, who studied us curiously. A young woman appeared from the kitchen to take our order.

We ordered Shan noodles. Two hot bowls of flat rice noodles seeped in clear chicken soup, topped with chopped tomatoes, crushed peanut, spinach leaves and spring onions, appeared shortly. A side dish of pickled mustard greens and bamboo shoots made our tongues tingle with the spicy sourness. It was a wonderful way to start the day and I could see that this dish could equally make a satisfying lunch or dinner. I pulled out my notepad and started to jot down the ingredients. The young woman noticed my interest and beckoned me to join her in the kitchen. I wished I had time to spend the whole day with her. There was so much to learn. She invited us to come back again so she could show me more Shan recipes. I thought this sounded like another book in the making!

stir-fried vermicelli

 | kyazun kyaw

When we were children, my brothers, sister and I would eagerly wait for our uncle to return from his evening stroll. He would always bring back a warm parcel of noodles. Wrapped in newspaper, the tangle of vermicelli flecked with an assortment of vegetables and meat were a welcome snack before it was time to get ready for bed.

ingredients

150g boneless chicken, cut into thin strips
1 teaspoon cornflour
½ teaspoon salt
½ teaspoon sugar
1 tablespoon light soy sauce
½ medium onion, thinly sliced lengthways
6 tablespoons peanut oil
100g baby corn, cut in half lengthways
50g green beans or mangetout, cut in half lengthways
100g carrots, cut into matchsticks
100g bean sprouts
1 egg, beaten
½ teaspoon salt
2 tablespoons light soy sauce
100g dried rice vermicelli
100ml water

method

Soak the vermicelli in cold water for 15 minutes until they are soft then drain well. Mix the cornflour, salt, sugar and soy sauce, then rub into the meat and leave for 10 minutes.

In the meantime, heat the oil in a wok, fry the sliced onions over a moderate heat until golden. Remove from the oil and drain on kitchen paper. To reduce the oiliness of the dish, spoon off some of the oil from the wok leaving about 2 tablespoons. Keep the removed oil for later use.

Return the wok to the heat, add the chicken and wait for a few seconds before tossing it. Stir fry for 2-3 minutes until the chicken is cooked. Transfer the meat to a plate and keep it warm. In the same wok, add all the vegetables except the bean sprouts. Toss these for a minute before adding the bean sprouts. Stir the vegetables for a further 30 seconds and season with salt.

Push the vegetables to the sides of the wok to form a well in the middle. Reduce the heat, and add the beaten egg and stir with a wooden spoon. When the egg is scrambled, mix in the vegetables. Remove half the mixture from the wok, and set to one side, keeping it warm. Return half of the cooked chicken, then pour in the soy sauce and water. As soon as the liquid is bubbling, add the vermicelli. Keep moving the vermicelli until all the liquid has been absorbed. Test the vermicelli to see if they are ready. If not add a tablespoon of water at a time and stir fry until cooked.

Finally add 1 tablespoon of the reserved onion oil and toss the noodles again. Check for seasoning and serve with the remaining fried vegetables and chicken piled on top. Sprinkle with crispy onions.

serves: 2
cooking time: 15-20 mins

tip
I always use brown rice vermicelli which tends to have a bit more bite. It is also much easier to handle. Even if you overcook it a little, it does not fall apart or clump together.

eat with
Spicy bean curd & peanut sauce ... p205

panthay noodles
 | panthay khaut swe

This is my version of Panthay noodles which originates from the Chinese Muslims in Burma. It's another great fusion of influences, stir-fried noodles with chicken masala. While I was in Rangoon, it was served with a fried egg on top so I have included this in the recipe.

ingredients
chicken masala on page 42
400g wheat noodles, cooked
100g white cabbage, shredded finely
2 tomatoes, chopped
2 tablespoons light soy sauce
1 tablespoon peanut oil
4 fried eggs

method
Follow the chicken masala recipe on page 42. When the chicken is done, cook the noodles according to the packet instructions. Have all the ingredients ready before assembling the dish as it takes little time.

Heat the oil in a wok, stir fry the cabbage and tomatoes for a minute or so until the cabbage is just cooked and the tomatoes are soft. Mix in the noodles and the sauce from the chicken masala. Toss the noodles until they are incorporated into all the ingredients. Finally season with soy sauce and serve the noodles with a portion of chicken topped with a fried egg.

serves: 4
cooking time: 10 mins, not including chicken masala

stir-fried noodles

ခေါက်ဆွဲကြော် | khaut swe kyaw

I love my mother's stir-fried noodles, and here's her secret. Firstly she never slices the cabbage but tears it by hand. It does have a different taste! And the other is that she adds the oil and sugar in the final stages of cooking so the noodles are not too oily and there is a hint of sweetness.

ingredients

½ medium onion, thinly sliced lengthways
6 tablespoons peanut oil
100g fresh shelled prawns
1 teaspoon cornflour
½ teaspoon salt
4 dried shiitake mushrooms
150g white cabbage, torn into pieces

100g carrots, sliced
50ml water
2 tablespoons light soy sauce
150g wheat noodles
1 teaspoon sugar
small handful of sliced spring onions

method

First rub the cornflour into the prawns and leave for 15 minutes. Soak the dried mushrooms in a bowl of hot water for 15 minutes. When they are soft and rehydrated, drain well and chop into slices. Cook the noodles following the packet instructions and prepare the vegetables before any stir frying takes place.

Heat the oil in a wok and fry the sliced onions over moderate heat until they are golden brown. Remove immediately from the oil and drain on kitchen paper. Pour some of the onion oil from the wok leaving only half the original amount. Reserve this oil for later use.

Return the wok to the heat and toss the prawns for 30 seconds until they are pink and opaque. Season with a pinch of salt and transfer to a small plate and leave to one side. Add the vegetables and mushrooms to the wok, and stir fry for a minute or so, adding a tablespoon of the onion oil if necessary. Season with a little salt, remove half the vegetables and set aside.

Add the water to the wok and wait for a minute or two until it is bubbling, then add the noodles and soy sauce. Toss the noodles until all the liquid has disappeared. Finally add sugar and 1 tablespoon of the onion oil, stir through the noodles then pile the fried vegetables and prawns on top. Check for seasoning and sprinkle with crispy onions and spring onions.

serves: 2
cooking time: 15-20 mins

variations

You also can use chicken or pork instead of prawns.

eat with

Pickled cucumber ... p212

festive duck noodle soup

ကော်ရည်ခေါက်ဆွဲ | kaw yea khaut swe

This recipe comes from one of my Aunt's family. Its origin is distinctly Chinese but it has evolved with influences from southeast Asian cooking. What really sets this noodle soup apart are the crunchy garnishes and the addictive tangy chilli paste! I find this hearty dish perfect for the weekend or for special occasions.

ingredients
½ duck
2 litres water
5cm fresh ginger, thickly sliced
2 tablespoons peanut oil
1 garlic clove, crushed
20g dried fish (bombay duck), soaked
    in hot water then shredded finely
1 tablespoon dark soy sauce
2 tablespoons light soy sauce
½ teaspoon ground black pepper
2 tablespoons cornflour
4 tablespoons water
1 egg, beaten
400g wheat noodles, cooked

garnishes
100g white radish, peeled & thinly sliced
½ small cucumber, thinly sliced
1 teaspoon salt
1 teaspoon sugar
½ lemon, juiced
100g bean sprouts
2 tablespoons peanut oil
5 garlic cloves, thinly sliced

chilli paste
15g shrimp paste
3 fresh red chillies
3 garlic cloves, leave skins on
1 lime, juiced

method
First prepare the chilli paste as this can be done well in advance. Set the oven at 180C/335F/Gas4. Wrap the shrimp paste in some foil and place on a baking sheet together with the garlic and red chillies, then roast for 15 minutes. Check the shrimp paste: it is ready when it has turned greyish in colour, and the texture is dry and crumbly. Peel the garlic and put into a pestle and mortar, add the chillies, discarding the stem, and shrimp paste, then pound until smooth. Add the lime juice and mix well then pour into a small bowl.

Next prepare the garnishes. Place the white radish slices in a small bowl, add ½ teaspoon of salt and set aside. After 15 minutes, drain and squeeze with your hands to remove as much liquid as possible. Return the radish to a bowl and add ½ teaspoon sugar and half the lemon juice. Do the same for the cucumber.

Boil a saucepan of water and blanch the bean sprouts for a minute until they have softened slightly, then drain and leave on one side. In a frying pan, heat 2 tablespoons of oil and fry the sliced garlic until golden. Remove with a slotted spoon and drain on kitchen paper.

Next start the soup. Remove any excess fat on the duck then place in a large saucepan full of water. Add the ginger and bring to the boil. Cover and simmer for 25-35 minutes until the duck is just cooked. Remove the duck from the pan and let it stand for 10 minutes or so until it is cool enough to handle. Strip the meat off the bone and shred into fine strips and set aside. Return the bones to the pan and simmer for another 30 minutes. The bones will help to further flavour the soup. In the meantime, heat the oil in a wok and stir fry the crushed garlic. Once it begins to turn golden, add the shredded dried fish and duck meat. Toss over moderate heat for a minute or so, then add both soy sauces and black pepper. Remove from heat and transfer to a bowl.

Finally, strain the soup, removing the bones and ginger, and return it to the heat. To thicken the soup, mix the cornflour with 4 tablespoons of water to form a smooth paste and add to the pan. Continue to stir for 5 minutes until the soup has thickened slightly. Add a quarter of the fried fish and duck, then stir in the beaten egg to create white ribbons in the soup. Season with salt and plenty of black pepper.

To serve, put a handful of noodles, some bean sprouts, fried duck and fish into a bowl and pour over the soup until the noodles are covered. Put the garnishes and chilli paste on the table and allow everyone to garnish as they wish.

serves: 6
cooking time: 80-90 mins

su's coriander noodles

 | nanan pyin khaut swe

If you have a bunch of fresh coriander in the fridge that needs to be used up, this is the perfect recipe. My sister's version is similar to an Italian pesto which can be made in advance and kept in the fridge for a few days. It's an instant meal mixed with any type of pasta or noodles.

ingredients
50g fresh coriander leaves
4 tablespoons peanut oil
2 garlic cloves
2 red chillies
1 lime, juiced

½ teaspoon sugar
2 tablespoons fish sauce
salt & black pepper
400g egg noodles or pasta

method
Make the garlic oil first. Slice a garlic clove and fry in the oil until golden. Remove from the oil and set aside. With a sharp knife finely chop the coriander, the remaining garlic clove and chillies. Place in a bowl and add the garlic oil, lime juice, sugar and fish sauce. Allow to infuse while cooking the noodles.

Cook the noodles according to the packet instructions. When you are ready to serve, toss the noodles with the coriander paste. Season with salt and pepper, and serve with crispy garlic sprinkled on top.

serves: 4
cooking time: 10 mins

eat with
Clear gourd soup ... p184

rice

burmese chicken biryani
ကြက်သားဒန်ပေါက် | kyet thar danbauk

At lunchtime the distinct aroma of fragrant rice and the promise of moist tender chicken draw a crowd to the danbauk stalls in the Indian quarters of Rangoon. I like to reserve this one-dish meal for the weekend so the rice can be left to slowly infuse with the spices. This version is light, not too rich or oily whilst retaining all the flavours. To complete the meal, serve with a fresh salad and minty yoghurt sauce.

ingredients

12 chicken pieces on the bone
6 tablespoons plain yoghurt
4 large onions, thinly sliced lengthways
peanut oil to fry onions
4 cardamom pods
4 cloves
1 cinnamon stick
2 teaspoons cumin seeds
2 teaspoons coriander seeds
½ teaspoon ground turmeric
1 teaspoon paprika

600g basmati rice
900ml water
a generous pinch of saffron threads
100g garden peas
85g cashew nuts
75g raisins
4 bay leaves
100g slightly salted butter, melted
3 teaspoons salt

method

Mix together one teaspoon of salt and yoghurt, then coat the chicken. Cover with cling film and leave to sit in the fridge for an hour or more. In the meantime, fry the onions in a generous amount of oil until golden brown. For best results, fry the onions in batches, see page 206 for crispy onions. Once the crispy onions are cool, crush them with your hands or chop them roughly.

In a dry saucepan or wok, roast the cardamom pods, cloves, cinnamon stick, cumin and coriander seeds on a low heat until they begin to smell fragrant. Grind the roasted spices in a pestle and mortar. Mix in the ground turmeric and paprika then combine with the crispy onions. Next put the rice, water and saffron in a saucepan. Cover, bring to the boil and simmer on a low heat until all the water has been absorbed, about 15 minutes. The rice should be cooked but still firm. Leave to cool while you prepare the remaining ingredients.

Butter the bottom of a large pan (approx. 5 litres capacity and preferably with a thick bottom). Add the chicken then spread a handful of the spiced crispy onions over the meat. Cover this with a quarter of the rice and sprinkle with another handful of crispy onions, and a third of the garden peas, cashew nuts and raisins. Repeat the layering process ending with a layer of rice.

Pop the bay leaves on top and pour over the melted butter. Cover the pan with a piece of foil and place the lid on top to ensure no moisture escapes. Cook over a very low heat for at least an hour until the flavours have infused with the rice and the chicken is cooked. You can test to see if it is ready by feeling the lid of the pan. If the lid is hot to the touch then it should be ready.

Remove the bay leaves, season with salt and stir through the rice. Serve the rice before carefully removing the chicken pieces from the bottom of the pan so that they don't fall apart.

serves: 6-8
cooking time: 1-2 hours

eat with
Danbauk salad ... p210
Minty yoghurt sauce ... p210
Pickled vegetables ... p211

golden sticky rice
ရွှေထမင်း | shwe htamin

The sticky rice is cooked with fried onions and turmeric turning it golden yellow. Traditionally, when a baby is one month old, the family marks the occasion by cooking golden sticky rice and coconut chicken curry. They then send the food to friends, family and neighbours. I like to eat the sticky rice on its own as a snack, sprinkled with shredded coconut, sesame seeds and crispy onions. My favourite bit is the rice stuck to the bottom of the pan which tends to be crispy and chewy.

ingredients
150g sticky/glutinous rice
2 tablespoons peanut oil
½ onion, thinly sliced lengthways
½ teaspoon turmeric
1 teaspoon salt
250ml water

method
First soak the rice in water for an hour, then rinse well and leave to drain in a sieve. Heat the oil in a saucepan and fry the sliced onions until they are beginning to turn golden, about 7-10 minutes. Add the turmeric and continue to fry for 30 seconds until it smells fragrant.

Add the rice, salt and water to the pan, and bring to the boil. Cover and simmer on a low heat for 15-20 minutes until the rice is cooked. Remove the pan from the heat and leave to rest for 5 minutes before serving. Taste and season as desired.

serves: 2-3
cooking time: 25-35 mins

eat with
Coconut chicken curry ... p45

burmese stir-fried rice

ထမင်းေကြာ် | htamin kyaw

This is an excellent way to use up leftover rice. It's quick and simple, something that I usually rustle up when our fridge is bare. I use the onion oil to fry the rice as this gives it a lovely aroma.

ingredients
½ small onion, thinly sliced lengthways
120ml peanut oil
1 egg, beaten
50g garden peas
300g cold cooked basmati rice
1 tablespoon light soy sauce
salt & black pepper
sliced spring onion for garnish

method
Heat the oil in a wok and add the sliced onions. Fry them over a moderate heat until golden, then remove from the oil and drain on kitchen paper.

Spoon some of the oil from the wok leaving about a tablespoon. Over a moderate heat, add the egg and stir with a wooden spoon until scrambled. Mix in the garden peas, soy sauce and rice.

Stir and toss the mixture, making sure every grain of rice is coated with the egg and oil. The key is to stir fry the rice long enough so that it has absorbed the oil and all the flavours from the other ingredients, about 3-5 minutes. My Aunt refers to this as 'until the rice begins to jump'. It is important to keep moving the rice in the wok otherwise it may burn and become hard.

Check for seasoning and sprinkle freshly ground black pepper, spring onions and crispy onions on top before serving.

serves: 2
cooking time: 10 mins

tip
To make the perfect fried rice, make sure the rice is completely cold before you begin to stir fry.

variations
This is a basic version to which I add prawns, chicken, pork or other vegetables for a more elaborate meal.

eat with
Dried shrimp relish ... p200
Lemon relish ... p198
Pickled cucumber ... p212

Shwedagon pagoda {part 2}

The air became thick with the heady smell of smouldering incense and the sweet scent of flowers as we reached the top of the stairs. On the main platform, we began the traditional route, walking clockwise around the stupa, and stopping at the pavilions to make offerings and donations. Occasionally we heard announcements on the tannoy or caught the soft chant of prayers from the monks. I followed my two older brothers and sister to look for our planetary posts while my parents sat in meditation.

In Burma the day of the week a person is born is of significance, as this will not only determine the first letter of their name, but also their planetary post which influences many aspects of daily life - from the selection of partners to days of the week when it is unlucky to cut your hair! There is a rhyme which we sang in the playground along the lines that a girl born on Friday should not marry a boy born on Monday. I never discovered why.

There are eight planetary posts as Wednesday is split into morning and afternoon. The posts are positioned at cardinal points around the pagoda. At the southwest corner,

we found a water seller, a slender young man tanned by the harsh sun. He gave me half a coconut shell to scoop up water from his container. With a shell-cup full of water, I squeezed through the crowd to my planetary post and poured water over the Naga, a mythical serpent which represents Saturday. I heard murmuring voices behind me saying, 'Let my head be as cool as this holy water. Let my worries be washed away with this clean water.'

We continued to walk around the pagoda, visiting each of our family's posts. By the time we had completed a full circuit, the sun had climbed high and the marble floor was already warm under our feet. Eventually we found our mother and father waiting for us at the eastern staircase. It was time to return home and we descended to the gate, sheltered from the increasing heat of the day.

butter & lentil rice

ပဲ၀ေထာပတ်ထမင်း | pe htaw bhut htamin

Rice is an essential part of a Burmese meal and on special occasions, like birthdays and anniversaries, we make butter and lentil rice to eat with rich meaty curries. The fragrant rice is a welcome alternative to plain rice. It can also be eaten on its own with some dried shrimp relish or crispy onions.

ingredients
200g basmati rice, rinsed and drained
1 tablespoon butter
35g split dried chana dal, soaked for 8 hours
½ teaspoon sugar
1 teaspoon salt
400ml water
2 bay leaves
1 cinnamon stick

method
Wash the chana dal and pick out any debris or dirt and drain well. In a saucepan, layer the rice then the chana dal. Add the remaining ingredients, cover and bring to the boil. Keep an eye on it so the rice doesn't bubble over.

Reduce the heat to low and simmer for 15-20 minutes until all the water has been absorbed and the dal is cooked. Leave to rest for 5 minutes before serving.

serves: 2-3
cooking time: 25 mins

tip
Yellow split peas are a good substitute for chana dal.

variations
Add a pinch of saffron threads to the rice before cooking to add colour and flavour.

eat with
Chicken masala ... p42
Pickled vegetables ... p211
Dried shrimp relish ... p200

sticky rice parcels

ကောက်ညှင်းထုပ် | kauknyin thouk

My mother's steaming bamboo leaf parcels, packed with sticky rice and all sorts of goodies, are like opening a present. Once you unwrap the leaf, the aromatic rice gives way to generous chunks of tender pork, golden salted egg yolks and other nuggets of flavours and textures. I must admit, one parcel is never enough!

ingredients
600g sticky/glutinous rice
3 tablespoons peanut oil
3½ tablespoons light soy sauce
1½ tablespoons dark soy sauce
2 teaspoons sugar
ground black pepper
16 bamboo leaves
string to tie the parcels

for the pork
225g pork, cut into cubes
½ tablespoon dark soy sauce
1 tablespoon light soy sauce
1 teaspoon sugar

for the fillings
4 tablespoons dried shrimps
4 dried shitake mushrooms
2 Chinese wind-dried sausages
100ml water
50g cooked chestnuts, peeled
2 boiled salted egg yolks (page 209)

method
Start by soaking the bamboo leaves in hot water until they are pliable. At the same time wash the rice and put into a large bowl, cover with water and soak for an hour. Put the dried mushrooms and dried shrimps in separate bowls of hot water and leave for 15 minutes or more.

Next prepare the pork. Put both soy sauces, sugar and pork in a saucepan. Cook over a moderate heat until the sugar has caramelised and any liquid that has come out of the meat has evaporated, about 2-3 minutes. Remove from the heat and set aside. Heat 100ml of water in a frying pan and add the Chinese sausages. Roll them around in the simmering water with a wooden spoon until the water has evaporated and the oil from the sausages is released. Remove from the pan and chop into pieces.

Drain the mushrooms, squeeze out any excess water and chop into small chunks. Heat ½ tablespoon of oil in a wok and stir fry the mushrooms for 1-2 minutes. Add ½ tablespoon light soy sauce, ½ tablespoon dark soy sauce and a pinch of freshly ground black pepper. Remove from the wok and set aside. In the same wok heat another ½ tablespoon of oil. Drain the dried shrimps and stir fry for a minute or so until they smell fragrant. Remove from the oil and leave to one side. Cut the salted egg yolks into quarters. Chop the chestnuts into small chunks.

Finally drain the rice. Heat the remaining 2 tablespoons of oil in a large saucepan and add the sugar. When the sugar has caramelised, add the rice and stir well. Mix in the remaining light and dark soy sauces, and cook for a couple of minutes. Season with a pinch of black pepper and remove from the heat to cool a little.

To assemble the parcels, pat the bamboo leaves dry. Divide the rice and all the filling ingredients into 8 portions. Take 2 bamboo leaves and fold into a cone. Stuff half of one rice portion into the cone. Next add the filling then cover with the remaining rice. Fold over the bamboo leaves to make a neat compact parcel and secure firmly with a string. In a large saucepan, boil enough salted water to cover the parcels. Place the parcels in the pan and simmer for at least 2 hours. Check occasionally to top up with water if necessary.

makes: 8
cooking time: 2-3 hours

eat with
Chilli sauce

tip
If bamboo leaves are unavailable, use foil and make rectangle parcels instead. Remember to pierce with a fork a couple of times on both sides to allow water to penetrate the rice.

coconut rice

အုန်းနို့ထမင်း | ohn nyot htamin

This coconut rice goes beautifully well with any type of Burmese curry. I sometimes serve the rice with slices of boiled egg, cucumber, green chillies and crispy onions. To help wash away the richness of the coconut, a sour soup or a salad completes the meal.

ingredients
200g basmati rice, rinsed and drained
150ml coconut milk
250ml water
1 small onion, sliced
1 tablespoon peanut oil
1 teaspoon salt

method
Put all the ingredients in a large saucepan, mix well and bring to the boil. Reduce the heat, then cover and simmer gently for 15-20 minutes until all the water has been absorbed. Do not remove the lid or stir the rice during this process. Switch the heat off and leave the rice to stand for 5 minutes before serving.

serves: 4
cooking time: 25 mins

eat with
Chicken curry ... p41
Sour white radish soup ... p187
Lemon relish ... p198

sticky rice with chicken
ကောက်ညှင်းကြက်သား | kauknyin kyet thar

My mother recalls this recipe with fondness. It was something she ate during the month after giving birth, known as the confinement period. During this time, it is customary for a mother to eat food that is considered 'hot' and this usually means something alcoholic and laden with ginger. For me this sticky rice is warming and comforting during the winter months when served with chicken soup.

ingredients
300g sticky/glutinous rice
2 tablespoons peanut oil
1cm fresh ginger, sliced
2 chicken thighs, skinned & boned then cut into 2cm cubes
1 tablespoon dark soy sauce
2 tablespoons light soy sauce
150ml Chinese rice wine
2 tablespoons black sesame oil
325ml water

method
First soak the rice in plenty of water for an hour, then rinse well and drain in a sieve. Heat the oil in a saucepan and fry the ginger for 30 seconds until it starts to smell fragrant. Add the chicken and cook for a further 2-3 minutes, lightly browning the meat. Mix in both soy sauces and continue to cook for a few more minutes before adding the rice and the remaining ingredients.

Stir well, cover with a lid and bring to the boil. Reduce the heat to the lowest setting and simmer gently for 20 minutes until the rice has absorbed all the liquid and the chicken is tender. Check for seasoning before serving.

serves: 4
cooking time: 30 mins

tip
You can use normal sesame oil if you cannot find black sesame oil, which has a more delicate flavour.

eat with
Cellophane noodle soup ... p190
Stir-fried & steamed vegetables ... p128

soups

red lentil soup

ပဲနီလေးဟင်းချို | pe neilay hincho

Most Burmese soups are served in small bowls as an accompaniment to the main meal. This soup is really simple to rustle up and a great way to use up any red lentils hiding in the back of the cupboard.

ingredients
30g red lentils
2 fresh ginger slices
500ml vegetable stock or water
2 tablespoons peanut oil
½ small onion, thinly sliced
¼ teaspoon ground turmeric
1 tablespoon fish sauce
fresh coriander to sprinkle on top
salt & pepper for seasoning

method
Put the red lentils, stock and ginger in a saucepan. Bring to the boil and simmer for 10-15 minutes until the lentils are tender, skim any scum off the top.

While the lentils are cooking, heat the oil in a small saucepan and fry the sliced onions until golden, about 5 minutes. Stir in the turmeric until it starts to smell fragrant. Pour the fried onions and oil into the lentils. Season with fish sauce and sprinkle with fresh coriander before serving.

serves: 2-4
cooking time: 15 mins

clear gourd soup

ဘူးသီးဟင်းခါး | budhi hingar

This is one of the easiest and quickest soups to throw together at the last minute. A bowl of this usually accompanies the Hand mixed salad. I like to add a generous amount of freshly ground black pepper which gives the soup a lovely warm kick.

ingredients

1 garlic clove, crushed and chopped
65g gourd, peeled, deseeded and sliced
1 teaspoon dried shrimps
500ml water
1 tablespoon fish sauce
½ teaspoon ground black pepper

method

Put all the ingredients in a saucepan and bring to the boil. Reduce heat and simmer for 10-15 minutes until the gourd is cooked but still retains its shape. Check for seasoning before serving.

serves: 2-4
cooking time: 15 mins

variations

Marrow or courgette works equally well if gourd is unavailable.

sour white radish soup

မုန်လာချဉ်ရည်ဟင်း | monlar chin yeahin

ingredients
100g white radish/daikon
2 tablespoons peanut oil
1 small onion, finely chopped
1 garlic clove, finely chopped
1 tablespoon dried shrimps
¼ teaspoon ground turmeric
20g tamarind pulp
100ml hot water
1 tomato, chopped
500ml vegetable stock or water
1 tablespoon fish sauce
small handful of fresh coriander, chopped

method
Peel the radish and cut into quarters along its length, then slice thinly. To prepare the tamarind, add hot water to the pulp and leave to soak for a few minutes to soften. Mash with a fork and strain through a sieve to remove any fibres or stones.

Heat the oil in a saucepan and cook the onion and garlic for 5 minutes, stirring from time to time. When the mixture is soft, mix in the turmeric and dried shrimps. Stir until the turmeric smells fragrant and then add the radish, tamarind liquid, tomato, fish sauce and stock. Bring to the boil and simmer for 15 minutes until the radish is cooked. Check for seasoning and sprinkle with coriander before serving.

serves: 2-4
cooking time: 20 mins

variations
If you want to make this a more substantial soup, add other vegetables like okra, egg-plant, green beans and potatoes.

cellophane noodle soup

ပဲကြာဇံဟင်းခါး | pe kyazan hingar

The knots of pale yellow lilies with their unique earthy flavour, the crunchy gelatinous black mushrooms, translucent noodles and ribbons of bean curd give this soup a distinctive Chinese flavour.

ingredients
35g cellophane noodles
4 dried wood-ear mushrooms
12 dried lily buds/golden needles
15g dried bean curd skin
10g dried shrimps
750ml chicken stock or water
1 tablespoon fish sauce
1 garlic clove, crushed
¼ teaspoon ground black pepper
spring onions for garnish

method
Soak the cellophane noodles, wood-ear mushrooms, lily buds and dried bean curd skin separately in bowls of warm water for 20 minutes until they soften. Drain and tie the lily buds into knots and trim any hard tips. Remove any grit from the wood-ear mushrooms and slice into strips. Similarly cut the bean curd skin into strips and the noodles in half, so they are more manageable.

In a saucepan, heat the stock and add all the ingredients. Simmer for 10 minutes until the noodles are translucent. Sprinkle with sliced spring onions. Check for seasoning and serve in small bowls as part of a meal.

serves: 4-6
cooking time: 15 mins

12 ingredient soup

၁၂ မျိုးဟင်းချို | setnit myo hincho

This soup is a great one to make when you have lots of vegetables in the fridge that need using up. You can vary the ingredients to whatever you like but I usually choose different textures and colours. It makes all the difference to start with a good stock so I tend to use an organic chicken.

ingredients
1 litre chicken stock
8 raw prawns, shelled
8 fish balls
3 dried wood-ear mushrooms
30g cellophane noodles
small tin of bamboo shoots
50g green beans
35g cauliflower
50g cabbage
1 carrot
1 egg, beaten
1 spring onion, thinly sliced
salt & black pepper

for the stock
½ chicken
1 onion
1 carrot
1 celery stick
1 bay leaf
plenty of water

method
Make the stock. Cut the chicken into manageable pieces, place in a large saucepan and cover with water. Roughly chop the onion, carrot and celery, and add to the pan along with the bay leaf. Bring to the boil, cover and simmer gently for 2 hours. Check occasionally to skim any scum off the top and add more water if the chicken is no longer submerged.

Remove the chicken and strain the stock into a clean saucepan. Once cooled, pop it in the fridge. Remove any fat that has congealed on the surface before using the stock. Strip the meat off the bone and cut into cubes to use in the soup.

Soak the wood-ear mushrooms and noodles in separate bowls of warm water for 10 minutes until they soften. Cut the mushrooms into shreds and the noodles into manageable lengths. Prepare the vegetables. Cut each vegetable so they are uniform in size to ensure similar cooking times.

To make the soup, pour a litre of chicken stock in a saucepan and bring to the boil, then simmer over moderate heat. Add the cooked chicken and the remaining ingredients except for the prawns, egg and spring onion. Continue to simmer for 10 minutes until the vegetables are tender but still have bite. Pop in the prawns and simmer for a couple of minutes until they are cooked.

Stir in the beaten egg and spring onion. Once the egg has turned into white ribbons, season with salt and black pepper. As this soup is more substantial than others, it can be served as a main dish.

serves: 4
cooking time: 30 mins, not including stock

tip
To make your own fish balls, follow the Fish cakes recipe (page 16) and instead of frying them, boil them in hot water as suggested in the variations.

lotus root & pork rib soup
ဝက်နံရိုးကြာရိုးဟင်းချို | wetnayo kya yoe hincho

ingredients
250g pork ribs
150g fresh lotus roots, peeled and sliced
750ml water
1 garlic clove, finely chopped
½ teaspoon salt
¼ teaspoon ground black pepper
1 teaspoon light soy sauce

method
Use a heavy sharp cleaver to cut the ribs into 5cm lengths. Alternatively have your butcher do this for you.

Heat a saucepan of water until boiling. Blanch the ribs in the water until they turn white. Remove them immediately and put into another saucepan. Discard the water. This process will remove some of the fat and scum that can build up, ensuring the soup remains clear.

Add the remaining ingredients to the pan, including 750ml of water, and return to the boil. Cover and simmer over moderate heat for 45 minutes until the meat is completely tender. Check for seasoning before serving.

serves: 4-6
cooking time: 50 mins

tip
Once you have peeled the lotus root, pop them into vinegared water to prevent discolouration until you are ready to use them.

condiments

lemon relish
သံပယိုသီးသုတ် | thambayo dhi thote

This is a version of shauk dhi thote using lemons. Shauk dhi is a type of citrus fruit found in Burma which has a delicate sourness. I think this relish goes particularly well with dried shrimp relish or as a side dish with any rich curry.

ingredients
1 large lemon
2 small shallots, thinly sliced lengthways
1 garlic clove, thinly sliced
3 tablespoons peanut oil
1 tablespoon fish sauce
½ teaspoon dried shrimps
1 teaspoon roasted chickpea powder (page 208)
dried chilli flakes

method
Put the sliced shallots into a bowl of cold water and soak for 5 minutes. In the meantime, heat the oil in a saucepan and fry the garlic until golden brown. Remove from the oil and drain on kitchen paper. Keep the oil for later.

Pound the dried shrimps in a pestle and mortar or blitz in a food processor until they resemble a coarse powder. The quality of the dried shrimps makes a huge difference as they give the relish a smoky flavour. Next prepare the lemon by cutting away the rind and separating into segments.

When you're ready to assemble the relish, drain the shallots, and squeeze out any excess water with your hands. Put into a small bowl, add the lemon segments, half of the garlic oil and the remaining ingredients. Mix well to make sure the shallots and lemon segments are coated with the dressing. Season with more fish sauce if it is too sharp; it should have a good balance of saltiness and sourness.

cooking time: 5 mins

variations
I also make this relish using pomelo when they are in season. You will need to break up the segments into smaller pieces and add a squeeze of lemon juice.

eat with
Dried shrimp relish ... p200
Burmese stir-fried rice ... p168

198

dried shrimp relish

 | ngapi kyaw

There are many versions of this dried shrimp relish, not only in Burma but throughout Asia. I am particularly fond of this version as it is as close as I can get to my Aunt's ngapi kyaw, which is just heavenly; crispy, spicy, salty with a hint of sweetness. Eat it on rice, toast, noodles - everything!

ingredients
200g dried shrimps
3 large onions, thinly sliced lengthways
10 garlic cloves, thinly sliced
250ml peanut oil
100g dried crushed chillies
15g shrimp paste
45g tamarind pulp
250ml hot water
½ teaspoon sugar

method
Wash the dried shrimps, drain and pat dry. Next, soak the tamarind in 200ml of hot water for a few minutes then mash with a fork. Strain the liquid through a sieve to remove fibres or stones and set aside. In another small bowl, add the shrimp paste and remaining 50ml of hot water, and work with a fork until smooth.

The shrimps need to be completely dry, so sometimes I help them along by putting them in an oven set at the lowest heat for a few minutes. Grind in a pestle and mortar until they resemble feather-like strands. It is fairly labour intensive but well worth it. However if you do not have the time or the muscle, blitz them in a food processor into a coarse powder.

Heat the oil in a saucepan and fry the onions in batches until golden. Remove from the heat and drain on kitchen paper. In the same oil, fry the garlic until golden and set aside. Spoon off half the oil from the pan and add the dried shrimps. Stir over a moderate heat for a minute or two and pour in the tamarind juice and shrimp paste liquid. Continue to stir the mixture for 15-20 minutes until all the liquid has evaporated, and the shrimps are dry and crispy. Add the dried chillies and sugar, and continue to cook until the chilli flakes have turned dark red, about 5 minutes. Remove from the heat and cool completely before mixing in the fried onions and garlic. Transfer to a jar with a lid and store in the fridge until needed. It will keep for a week or two, although it rarely lasts that long in our house.

cooking time: 45 mins

eat with
Burmese stir-fried rice ... p168
Stir-fried & steamed vegetables ... p128

sour chilli dip

အချဉ်ရည် | achin yea

ingredients
1 lemon or 2 limes, juiced
3 green chillies, thinly sliced
1 garlic clove, crushed and finely chopped
1 teaspoon fresh coriander, chopped
fish sauce to taste

method
Mix together the lemon or lime juice with crushed garlic and green chillies. Add a teaspoon of fish sauce at a time until it tastes salty and sour. Sprinkle the chopped coriander and serve as a dip with fritters.

cooking time: 5 mins

tip
For a less spicy version, remove the white pith from the green chillies as this is the hottest part.

eat with
Pea crackers... p11
Fish cakes ... p16
Pumpkin & shrimp cake ... p32

soy sauce dip

ပဲငံပြာရည် | pe nanpya yea

ingredients
3 tablespoons light soy sauce
1 garlic clove, crushed and finely chopped
½ lime, juiced
¼ teaspoon sugar
2 green chillies, sliced

method
Simply mix all the ingredients together in a small bowl. Check for seasoning, it should be salty, sour and spicy.

cooking time: 5 mins

eat with
Boiled crab ... p78
Marinated pork skewers ... p13
Pumpkin & shrimp cake ... p32

tamarind dip

မန်ကျည်းရည် | magyi yea

ingredients
30g tamarind pulp
150ml hot water
1 garlic clove
½ teaspoon salt
½ teaspoon sugar
2 green chillies, sliced (optional)
1 teaspoon fresh coriander, chopped

method
Add the hot water to the tamarind and soak for 5-10 minutes. When the pulp has softened, mash with a fork and strain through a sieve to remove any fibres or stones.

Grind the garlic, salt and sugar in a pestle and mortar, then mix with the tamarind liquid. It should be salty, sour and slightly sweet. Finally add the chillies and coriander.

cooking time: 5-10 mins

eat with
Crispy fritters... p21
Shrimp & bean sprout cups ... p29
Yellow split pea fritters ... p12

crispy garlic & oil

 | cek thun pyu kyaw – si

ingredients
5 garlic cloves, thinly sliced
peanut oil

method
Pour enough oil in a small saucepan to deep fry the garlic. It should be about a quarter full. It is important that all the garlic should be sliced equally thick as this will ensure it cooks evenly and at the same time.

When the oil is hot, add the garlic and stir to separate the slices. Fry until they are beginning to turn golden, immediately remove with a slotted spoon, then drain on kitchen paper. They will continue to cook a little more and will be perfectly golden and crispy.

The garlic oil can be used in salads or to stir fry vegetables. Store any excess oil in a clearly labelled jar so it can be reused to make more crispy garlic.

cooking time: 5 mins

spicy bean curd & peanut sauce

ပဲပုပ်ခရန်းချဉ်သီးခြေမြပဲ | tou kyu khayan chin dhi maype

ingredients
2 tablespoons peanut oil
½ small onion, sliced lengthways
1 tablespoon fermented chilli bean curd
1 large tomato, finely chopped
handful of roasted unsalted peanuts, chopped
1 tablespoon lemon juice

method
To make the crispy onions, heat the oil in a saucepan and fry the sliced onions until golden, then remove from the oil and drain on kitchen paper.

Reduce the heat, add the tomato to the pan and simmer for 5 minutes until softened. Mix in the fermented bean curd, work with a wooden spoon until dissolved in the to-mato sauce. Taste a bit of the sauce to see if it needs seasoning. I find the bean curd is usually salty enough.

Finally add the chopped peanuts, crispy onions and lemon juice. Mix well and serve in a small bowl.

cooking time: 15 mins

tip
There are two types of fermented bean curd: the white bean curd usually comes in a chilli brine and is the one used here; the other is the red bean curd and is mainly used in meat dishes.

eat with
Stir-fried vermicelli ... p152
Burmese stir-fried rice ... p168
Stir-fried & steamed vegetables ... p128

crispy onions & oil

 | cek thun ni kyaw – si

ingredients
2 medium onions, thinly sliced lengthways
1 teaspoon salt
peanut oil

method
When slicing the onions, ensure they are the same thickness so they cook evenly. I use a mandoline to do this. Put the onions in a bowl and sprinkle with the salt, mix thoroughly and leave to stand for 15 minutes. This will draw out water from the onions and help to make them crispy when they are fried.

Roll the onions up in kitchen paper and squeeze to remove any excess water. Pour the oil in a saucepan until a third full and when hot, gently drop in a quarter of the onions and stir to separate the slices. Turn the onions with a fork regularly and fry until golden, about 7-10 minutes. Watch carefully during the frying process as the onions can turn quickly and become burnt.

Remove the onions with a slotted spoon and spread on kitchen paper. Once they have cooled, they should be very crisp. Continue to fry the onions in batches. Use immediately or store in a glass jar with a tight-fitting lid and keep in the fridge.

The onion oil can be used in salads or to stir fry vegetables or rice. Store any excess oil in a clearly labelled jar so it can be reused at a later date.

cooking time: 40 mins

fried crispy noodles

 | kyauk swe ajewt kyaw

ingredients
large handful of rice noodles
peanut oil

method
Pour the oil into a small saucepan, about a third of the way up. When it is hot, drop a few uncooked noodles into the oil. They will puff up and float to the top, after about 5 seconds. Immediately remove from the oil with a slotted spoon and continue to fry the remaining noodles in small batches. Drain on kitchen paper and cool.

cooking time: 5 mins

baked shrimp paste dip

ငါးပိဖွတ် | ngapi daung

My aunties refer to this as Burmese butter. A small bowl of this with an assortment of raw vegetables is served at most meals.

ingredients
25g shrimp paste
2 red chillies
3 garlic cloves, unpeeled
2 limes, juiced
1 tablespoon dried shrimps, pounded into floss

method
Set the oven at 180°C/350°F/Gas4. Wrap the shrimp paste in foil and place on a baking sheet. Roast for 5 minutes then add the garlic and chillies to the sheet and continue to bake for a further 10-15 minutes until the shrimp paste is dry and greyish in colour. Remove from the oven and leave to cool.

Peel the skins off the garlic and remove the stems from the chillies and place them in a pestle and mortar. Add the baked shrimp paste and dried shrimps then pound the mixture until all the ingredients are well incorporated. Stir in the lime juice to form a runny paste. Transfer to a small bowl and serve with an assortment of vegetables to dip in the sauce. If you find the dip a bit too sour season with a little salt.

cooking time: 20 mins

eat with
An assortment of vegetables – cucumber, carrots, celery, small round eggplants etc.

roasted chickpea powder

 | pe mote

As the name suggests, this is made from ground chickpeas and has a slightly grainy texture. When roasted, it has a nutty, earthy flavour.

ingredients
150g chickpea powder

method
Pour the powder into a large frying pan and dry roast over a moderate heat, stirring with a wooden spoon for 2-3 minutes until the powder has turned a shade darker. Remove from the heat and pour into a bowl to cool before transferring to a jar for storage.

cooking time: 5 mins

salted eggs

ဆားရည်စိမ်ဘဲဥ | sar yea sain beh u

ingredients
250g salt
2 litres water
6 duck eggs (or hen eggs)

method
Bring a pan of water to the boil. Stir in the salt until it has fully dissolved. Remove from the heat and leave to cool completely.

Find a glass jar or a plastic container large enough to accommodate the brine and the eggs. Place the eggs inside the jar and pour the brine over the top, making sure all the eggs are completely submerged. Replace the lid, label with the date and leave in a cool dark place for 3-4 weeks.

After curing, remove the eggs from the jar and keep them in the fridge if not using immediately. They should keep in the fridge for 2-3 months, however they will continue to cure and become saltier. The yolk should be a bright yellow-orange and set, while the egg white remains cloudy.

To hard boil the eggs, pop into a saucepan and cover with cold tap water. Bring to a rolling boil and simmer for 10-15 minutes. Drain them and immediately place in a bowl of iced water. This will make peeling a lot easier.

cooking time: 10-15 mins

related recipes
Sticky rice parcels... p174
Minced pork & salted egg ... p70

minty yoghurt sauce

ပူဇိနာ ဒိန်ချဉ် | puthe nan dane chin

ingredients
500g plain or Greek-style yoghurt
large handful of fresh mint, chopped
½ teaspoon paprika
salt

method
Pour the yoghurt into a bowl, add the mint leaves and paprika. Season with salt.

cooking time: 2 mins

eat with
Burmese chicken biryani ... p166
Potato & lamb cutlets ... p25

danbauk salad

သီးစုံသုပ် | dhi sone thote

ingredients
½ cucumber, deseeded and diced
3 medium tomatoes, diced
½ red onion, thinly sliced
handful of mint leaves, chopped
handful of fresh coriander, chopped
½ lemon, juiced
salt & freshly ground black pepper

method
Just before serving, toss all the ingredients in a bowl. Season with salt and pepper.

cooking time: 5 mins

eat with
Burmese chicken biryani... p166

pickled vegetables

သီးစုံသနပ် | dhi sone thanut

ingredients
1 teaspoon coriander seeds
1 teaspoon cumin seeds
1 cinnamon stick
½ teaspoon ground turmeric
½ teaspoon mustard seeds
1 teaspoon chilli powder
1 small cauliflower
2 carrots
4-6 small garlic cloves
50ml wine vinegar
2 tablespoons peanut oil
2 teaspoons sugar
2 teaspoons salt

method
Wash and cut the vegetables into bite-sized pieces. Set aside to drain on kitchen paper. The pickled vegetables will keep longer if they are very dry. To help them along, pop them in an oven at the lowest setting for about 5 minutes. Transfer the vegetables to a bowl, add the vinegar, sugar and salt, and leave to marinate for 10 minutes.

In the meantime prepare the spices by dry roasting in a wok over low heat for a minute or two. When they smell fragrant, remove from the heat and put into a pestle and mortar, and grind into powder.

Heat the oil in a saucepan and cook the spices for a minute to flavour the oil. Remove from the heat and pour over the vegetables, and mix thoroughly. Leave to cool before refrigerating. They are best eaten after 2 days when the vegetables have become infused with the spices but are still fresh and crunchy.

cooking time: 10 mins

eat with
Burmese chicken biryani... p166
Butter & lentil rice ... p173

chilli & dried shrimp oil

ငရုပ်ဆီ | ngayouk si

ingredients
50g dried red chilli flakes
2 tablespoons dried shrimps, pounded into floss
150ml peanut oil

method
Heat the oil in a heavy saucepan and add the dried chilli flakes. Stir frequently and cook until the chillies are just beginning to turn dark red/brown in colour. Keep a close eye on them as the chillies can burn quickly. Mix in the dried shrimps and stir for a further minute then remove from the heat.

Carefully pour into a sterilized heat-resistant jar with a tight-fitting lid. Cool completely before storing in the fridge. The oil will keep for a few months.

cooking time: 5 mins

pickled cucumber

သခွါးသီးသနပ် | tha hkaw dhi thanut

ingredients
1 small cucumber
1 teaspoon salt
1 lime, juiced
1 teaspoon sesame seeds, toasted
1cm fresh ginger, thinly sliced
2 garlic cloves, thinly sliced
2 green chillies, thinly sliced
1 teaspoon sugar
1 tablespoon peanut oil
¼ teaspoon ground turmeric

method
Thinly slice the cucumber and put into a bowl, then sprinkle with salt. After 10 minutes, discard any liquid in the bowl and wrap the cucumber with kitchen paper. Squeeze to extract any remaining liquid. Return the cucumber to the bowl and add the lime juice, sesame seeds, ginger, garlic, green chillies and sugar.

Heat the oil in a small saucepan, add the turmeric and cook for a minute until the oil is fragrant. Cool the oil before adding to the cucumber. Mix well and refrigerate until needed.

cooking time: 10 mins

sweet snacks

golden semolina pudding

ရွှေကြည်ဆန္ဆန္နင်းမကင်း | shwegyi sanwei makin

I think this is a great way to eat semolina, rich and moist in the middle and crunchy on top. It always goes down well at the end of a meal with a splash of cream and if there are any leftovers, have it with a cup of tea the next day.

ingredients
350g semolina (preferably coarse grain)
350g caster sugar
400ml coconut milk
1 teaspoon salt
2 large eggs, beaten
600ml water
125ml peanut oil
1 tablespoon white poppy seeds

method
Pour the semolina on to a baking sheet or frying pan and roast over moderate heat or under the grill for 5-10 minutes. Stir frequently until the semolina has turned golden brown. Watch carefully so it does not burn. Remove from the heat and pour into a large saucepan.

Mix in the remaining ingredients, except the poppy seeds. Use a whisk to remove any lumps. Over a moderate heat bring the mixture to the boil, stirring continuously. Soon you will notice the mixture beginning to thicken and at the first sign of bubbles appearing, turn down the heat to the lowest setting.

You need to stir continuously throughout the cooking process. As the mixture becomes thicker, it can be hard work. I find it useful to recruit an extra pair of hands in the kitchen to help. Continue to simmer very gently for 8-10 minutes until the mixture starts to clump together and comes away from the sides of the pan easily.

Pour the mixture into a cake tin or an oven-proof dish, approximately 22cm in diameter, which has been greased with oil. Smooth over the surface with the back of a spoon so it is level. Sprinkle the poppy seeds and place under a hot grill for 8-10 minutes until the top is golden and some cracks appear on the surface. Serve at room temperature.

serves: 10-12
cooking time: 30-40 mins

tip
You can make this in advance as it will keep in the fridge for up to 5 days. Before serving, just pop it in the microwave for 10 seconds to take the chill off.

variations
Add a pinch of ground cardamom or nutmeg for an aromatic Indian influence or add a small handful of raisins or chopped roasted almonds to the cooked mixture before pouring into the tin.

coconut agar jelly

ကျောက်ကျော် | kyauk geor

What I love about this sweet jelly is that it's easy to make and looks impressive: the coconut milk separates and sets to form two layers, the top is white and the bottom is translucent. The agar agar sets the jelly without refrigeration and does not melt in hot weather making it perfect for summer.

ingredients
10g agar agar strands
350ml fresh coconut milk
350ml water
85g caster sugar
¼ teaspoon salt

method
First soak the agar agar in a bowl of water for 10 minutes until softened. Drain and cut the strands in half and pop into a saucepan. Add the coconut milk and water to the pan and bring to the boil. Simmer over moderately high heat, stirring frequently and keeping a close eye so it does not bubble over. Cook until all the agar agar strands have completely dissolved, about 15-20 minutes. Turn the heat off, add the sugar and salt, stirring until both are completely dissolved.

Pour into a container, approximately 17cm x 12cm x 5cm, let it set at room temperature, then cover and refrigerate. The jelly will stay fresh and moist for several days if covered in 1cm of cold water. Cut into diamonds or slices and serve. It should be firm enough to pick up with your fingers.

serves: 6-8
cooking time: 25 mins

tip
Using fresh coconut milk really makes a difference. To make this yourself, remove the coconut from the shell and peel the brown skin. Cut the flesh into small chunks and place in a blender. Add 250ml of warm water and blitz until the coconut is finely shredded. Leave for a few minutes to soak.

Place a sieve covered with a piece of muslin cloth over a bowl and pour in the coconut mixture. Twist the muslin cloth into a ball and squeeze as hard as you can to extract the liquid. It should make about 350ml of thick coconut milk.

avocado ice cream

ေထာပတ်သီးရေခဲမုန့် | htaw hbut dhi yea kare mot

The literal translation for avocado in Burmese is butter fruit. Avocados always remind me of a treat we used to eat in Burma and one that I particularly enjoy, an avocado smoothie. It was simply made with a ripe avocado, milk, a little condensed milk and sugar, resulting in a rich frothy drink. I have adapted this recipe into an ice cream which can be served as a dessert or a treat any time of day.

ingredients
1 large avocado, very ripe
25g caster sugar
1 tablespoon milk
120ml double cream

method
Scoop the flesh of the avocado into a liquidiser, add the milk and sugar then blend until smooth. Stir the cream into the mixture then pour into an ice cream maker, churn and freeze.

If you don't have an ice cream maker, pour the cream into a mixing bowl and whip until it forms soft peaks. Fold the avocado mixture into the cream and pour into a shallow plastic container. Freeze for 3-4 hours, stirring occasionally.

serves: 2, generously
cooking time: 5 mins

tip
Remove from the freezer 10 minutes before serving.

variations
I found adding the seeds of a vanilla pod or a little lime juice for a hint of citrus really works well.

festival sticky rice

ထမင်း | htamane

This is usually made during the harvest festival in February. Similar to semolina pudding, it requires continuous stirring throughout the cooking process and can be hard work. Well worth recruiting a few people to help in the kitchen. Although considered a sweet snack by Burmese standards, it does not contain any sugar but has fresh coconut, peanuts and sesame seeds to add flavour and texture.

ingredients
250g sticky/glutinous rice
750ml water
1 teaspoon salt
3 tablespoons peanut oil
2cm fresh ginger, shredded finely
35g roasted unsalted peanuts, chopped
4 tablespoons sesame seeds, toasted
large handful of fresh grated coconut

method
First rinse the rice, then put into a large bowl and cover with water. Soak for an hour before draining. Heat the oil in a saucepan and fry the ginger for 30 seconds to flavour the oil. Add the rice, water and salt. Bring to the boil and reduce the heat.

Simmer gently for 20-30 minutes until all the water has been absorbed by the rice. Throughout the cooking process, it is important to stir continuously, otherwise the rice will not have a smooth creamy texture when it breaks down into a paste.

Remove from the heat and sprinkle with peanuts, sesame seeds and coconut. Fold into the rice and serve warm.

serves: 4-6
cooking time: 35 mins

caramelised crispy pancakes

မုန့်ဆီကြော် | mote si kyaw

This is a sweet crispy sticky golden pancake that reminds me of brandy snaps. The pancakes are extremely soft and sticky during cooking and transform into chewy caramelised discs when they are cool.

ingredients
60g sticky/glutinous rice flour
20g rice flour
125ml water
100g palm sugar (or brown sugar)
4 tablespoons water
peanut oil for shallow frying

method
Put both flours in a mixing bowl, mix in the water to form a thick batter. Leave to rest for 20 minutes while preparing the sugar.

If you are using palm sugar, grate it before placing in a small saucepan. Add 4 table-spoons of water and over moderate heat stir until the sugar has completely dissolved. Remove from the heat and allow the sugar to cool. Gradually pour the sugar into the batter to form a consistency similar to single cream.

When you are ready to fry the pancakes, heat enough oil to shallow fry in a small non-stick frying pan. Spoon a small ladle of batter into the oil and swirl the batter in the pan to form a circular shape.

Leave the pancake over moderate heat until the edges are golden brown, then carefully flip over and cook the other side. When it is golden brown on both sides, remove from the heat and cool on a plate. The pancake remains soft and sticky until it is cool. Repeat this process making one pancake at a time until all the batter is used up, replenishing the oil when necessary.

makes: 10-12 pancakes
cooking time: 50 mins

new year rice dumplings
မုန့်လုံးရေပေါ် | mon lone yea paw

This is a sweet snack made during the water festival, Thingyan, in mid-April to mark the lunar new year. People, young and old, throw water over each other to celebrate and welcome the new year by washing away bad luck. It's also a time when family and friends get together and the kitchen is bursting with aunties making rice dumplings and other elaborate meals.

ingredients
75g sticky/glutinous rice flour
35g rice flour
¼ teaspoon salt
100ml cold water
20g palm sugar (or brown sugar)
½ fresh coconut, grated

method
Put both flours and salt in a mixing bowl, then add the water and stir with a spoon until everything comes together. The mixture should feel dry but form a ball when a handful of it is rolled in the palms. If it is too dry, add a little extra water. Next, grate or cut the palm sugar into small pieces prior to making the dumplings.

Roughly divide the mixture into 12 portions, roll each into a ball. Push with a finger to form a small hollow in the centre and put ½ teaspoon of palm sugar inside. Seal the hole by squeezing the mixture together again and rolling in the palms to reshape into a ball. Put the dumplings on a piece of cling film so they don't stick to the work surface.

Bring a saucepan of water to the boil and pop half the dumplings into the boiling water and simmer for 3-5 minutes, uncovered. When the balls have floated to the top, they are cooked. Remove with a slotted spoon. Cook the remaining dumplings as before and serve them warm sprinkled with freshly grated coconut.

makes: 12 dumplings
cooking time: 10 mins

Full moon in Kason

May (Kason) is the second month of the year according to the Burmese calendar. During Kason, unique to our street in Rangoon, a festival was held to celebrate the triple-blessed day and the full moon of Kason. On this particular day, in different years of his life, Buddha was born, gained enlightenment and passed away attaining nirvana. This festival was an important religious event and every year my mother and her sisters prepared robes to offer to monks. Our kitchen became a hive of activity with aunties, uncles and cousins all helping with the preparations.

My favourite part of any festival was undoubtedly the food, particularly Burmese cakes and other specialities. One of my favourite is Golden semolina pudding (shwegyi sanwei makin). My Aunt Eng made large trays of the pudding, recruiting a few of the older children to help her stir the mixture over a charcoal stove as the semolina thickened. When the pudding was cooked, slices of the rich moist semolina were consumed with sweet milky tea.

With a satisfied stomach, I remembered sitting with the other children on bamboo mats, rolled out on the street in front of the pavilion where a stage was set up for the evening entertainment. Loud music blared out, girls dressed in intricate costumes danced to traditional music before the pantomimes began. I was allowed to stay up late to enjoy the festival which tended to go on until the early hours of the morning, although for most of it I was happily curled up asleep on the mat next to my big sister.

burmese faluda

ဖာလူဒါ | paluda

This is a much-loved dessert/drink that is best described as a sort of sundae: layers of yellow egg pudding, rose pink sago pearls, green threads of cendol and glossy cubes of agar jelly are all drenched in chilled milk, topped with ice cream. What a great way to cool off and indulge yourself on a hot summer afternoon.

for the egg pudding
2 eggs
1 egg yolk
250ml milk
15g sugar
small pinch of salt

for the sago pearls
50g sago, medium pearls
a drop of pink colouring (optional)
plenty of water

for the cendol
10 pandan leaves, finely chopped
75g green pea flour
250ml water
¼ teaspoon edible alkaline water or lye water

and also
coconut agar jelly, halve the recipe on page 219
4 teaspoons rose syrup
600ml full fat milk, chilled
4 scoops vanilla ice cream

method
I usually make the coconut agar jelly a day in advance, remembering to halve the original quantities.

Make the egg pudding. Preheat the oven to 160C/315F/Gas2. Grease an oven-proof dish, about 20cm x 10cm, with a little oil. In a bowl, whisk together the eggs, egg yolk, sugar and salt. Heat the milk in a saucepan for a few minutes so it is just warm and slowly pour into the eggs, stirring to combine. Transfer the egg mixture to the dish and place in the oven. Bake for 25-30 minutes until the custard is set and the top is golden brown. Remove from the oven and leave to cool. Cover with cling film and transfer to the fridge until needed.

While the pudding is baking, make the sago. Boil a saucepan of water and add the sago when the water is boiling. Simmer for 20-25 minutes until the sago pearls are almost transparent all the way through. Stir the mixture continually to avoid burning. Pop a lid on, turn off the heat and leave for 10 minutes to allow the residual heat to cook the sago through so the pearls are totally transparent. Pour into a sieve, rinse under cold water and transfer into a bowl. Mix in the pink colouring until all the sago pearls are coated. Chill in the fridge until needed.

To make the cendol, pound the pandan leaves with 50ml of water in a pestle and mortar or blitz in a blender. Strain the mixture through a fine sieve or muslin cloth. Add the pandan liquid to the green pea flour and mix in the remaining 200ml of water and alkaline water. Leave to soak for 1 hour.

Transfer the green pea mixture to a thick-bottomed saucepan and cook over moderate heat, stirring constantly. Continue to stir until the mixture has thickened and become glossy. Over a large bowl of iced water, push the mixture through a cendol maker or colander with quick short strokes of a wooden spoon. Leave the cendol pieces to set in the cool water for about 10 minutes. Then drain and rinse the pieces to prevent them from sticking together.

To serve, cut the egg pudding and agar jelly into small pieces. Put a teaspoon of rose syrup into each tall glass and add a portion of each filling, then pour in the milk so that it is three-quarters of the way up. Finally float a scoop of ice cream on top.

serves: 4
cooking time: 1-2 hours

tamarind sorbet
မန်ကျည်းရေခဲ | magyi yea kare

Tamarind pulp is made into a sweet and sour drink in Burma called magyi pyao yea. Here I have turned it into a sorbet, a refreshing way to end a meal when served with some fresh fruit.

ingredients
750ml water
75g tamarind pulp
100g palm sugar (or brown sugar)
½ teaspoon salt

method
Put the water and tamarind in a saucepan. Bring to the boil and simmer for 2-3 minutes. Stir in the sugar and salt then remove from the heat. Strain through a sieve or muslin cloth to remove any fibres or stones.

Pour the mixture into a shallow plastic container, ensuring the mixture is no deeper than 3cm so that it freezes quickly. Place in a freezer and stir every 2 hours with a fork to break up the ice crystals. Repeat this two or three times until the mixture is light and fluffy but still grainy.

serves: 6
cooking time: 5-10 mins

index

About the author

Tin Cho Chaw

Born in Rangoon (Yangon), I grew up surrounded by a family of enthusiastic cooks. Aged 8, my life changed completely when I arrived in the UK unable to speak a word of English. Growing up in a quiet town in Devon, I missed the familiar, comforting food of my childhood. This was when I began to develop a keen interest in cooking Burmese food.

After years of experimenting and calling my mother for instructions, I began to write down and record our family recipes.

In 2004 I returned to Burma. Travelling through the country and staying with family allowed me to taste the authentic flavours and see the techniques that cannot be learnt from living so far away.

Since then I have been refining these recipes which have become part of my everyday cooking.

For additional information, videos and other resources, visit: www.hsaba.com.

Acknowledgements

Special thanks to:
Amy, Christopher, Aung, Tom, Su, Jon, Khin Khin Lat, Myint Han, Chris Wood, Martin Hopkins, Christian McDonald, Steven Chou, Rita and everyone involved in the making of this book.